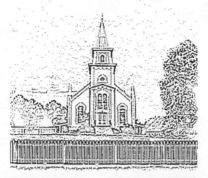

CHARLES SPURGEON

~ *Christian Living Classics* ~

THE POWER OF CHRIST'S SECOND COMING

~ Compiled and Edited by LANCE WUBBELS ~

Emerald Books

P.O. Box 635
Lynnwood, Washington 98046

Scripture quotations are taken from the King James Version of the Bible.

The Power of Christ's Second Coming
Copyright © 1996
Lance C. Wubbels

Published by Emerald Books
P.O. Box 635
Lynnwood, WA 98046

ISBN 1-883002-20-6

Printed in the United States of America.

About the Author

CHARLES HADDON SPURGEON (1834–1892) was the remarkable British "Boy Preacher of the Fens" who became one of the truly greatest preachers of all time. Coming from a flourishing country pastorate in 1854, he accepted a call to pastor London's New Park Street Chapel. This building soon proved too small and so work on Spurgeon's Metropolitan Tabernacle was begun in 1859. Meanwhile his weekly sermons were being printed and having a remarkable sale—25,000 copies every week in 1865 and translated into more than twenty languages.

Spurgeon built the Metropolitan Tabernacle into a congregation of over 6,000 and added well over 14,000 members during his thirty-eight-year London ministry. The combination of his clear voice, his mastery of language, his sure grasp of Scripture, and a deep love for Christ produced some of the noblest preaching of any age. An astounding 3,561 sermons have been preserved in sixty-three volumes, *The New Park Street Pulpit* and *The Metropolitan Tabernacle Pulpit*, from which the chapters of this book have been selected and edited.

During his lifetime, Spurgeon is estimated to have preached to 10,000,000 people. He remains history's most widely read preacher. There is more available material written by Spurgeon than by any other Christian author, living or dead. His sixty-three volumes of sermons stand as the largest set of books by a single author in the history of Christianity, comprising the equivalent to the twenty-seven volumes of the ninth edition of the *Encyclopedia Britannica*.

About the Editor

LANCE WUBBELS is the managing editor of Bethany House Publishers. His interest in the writings of Charles Spurgeon began while doing research on an editorial project that required extensive reading of Spurgeon's sermons. He discovered a wealth of sermon classics that are filled with practical, biblical insight for every believer and written in a timeless manner that makes them as relevant today as the day they were spoken. His desire is to select and present Spurgeon's writings in a way that will appeal to a wide audience of readers and allow one of the greatest preachers of all time to enrich believers' lives.

Wubbels is the author of *The Gentle Hills* fiction series with Bethany House Publishers, a four-book series that is set during World War II, as well as the heartwarming short novel, *One Small Miracle*. A naturally gifted storyteller, he captures readers with a warm, homey style filled with wit and insight that appeals to a wide readership.

Contents

CHARLES SPURGEON
CHRISTIAN LIVING CLASSICS

Grace Abounding in a Believer's Life

A Passion for Holiness in a Believer's Life

The Power of Prayer in a Believer's Life

Spiritual Warfare in a Believer's Life

The Triumph of Faith in a Believer's Life

What the Holy Spirit Does in a Believer's Life

The Power of Christ's Miracles

The Power of Christ's Prayer Life

The Power of Christ's Second Coming

The Power of Christ's Tears

The Power of Christ the Warrior

The Power of the Cross of Christ

F.B. MEYER
CHRISTIAN LIVING CLASSICS

Abraham: The Obedience of Faith

David: Shepherd, Psalmist, King

Joseph: Beloved, Hated, and Exalted

Moses: The Servant of God

Paul: A Servant of Jesus Christ

Peter: Fisherman, Disciple, Apostle

Introduction

BOOKS ON THE SECOND COMING of Jesus Christ abound today, and throughout the many centuries of the Church's history, Christ's second coming has been a theme that has greatly edified believers all around the world. It has also given rise to many strange and speculative teachings—often controversial, sometimes heretical. It is unfortunate that this great biblical teaching, so full of comfort and hope for the believer, should be so often maligned and used by certain teachers to gain a following and perhaps be the means to selling a lot of books.

As one of the greatest expository preachers of all time, Charles Spurgeon is eminently qualified to teach on the second coming of Christ. His amazing thirty-eight-year metropolitan ministry in the city of London during the 1800s marked an era of some of the most gifted pastors ever assembled in Great Britain—Joseph Parker, H. P. Liddon, Hugh Price Hughes, F. B. Meyer, R. W. Dale, Alexander Maclaren, Alexander Whyte, F. W. Farrar. But in the matter of the influence of the gospel—both in large audiences and through the printed page—none matched Spurgeon's contribution. His ministry was said to be unparalleled in England since the days of Whitefield and Wesley.

The quintessential Victorian Englishman whose masterful preaching astonished his generation gives us these words of instructions on how he approached the biblical theme of Christ's second coming: "It is rare that I intrude into the mysteries of the future with regard to either the second coming, the millennial reign, or the first and second resurrection. As often as I come across it in my expositions, I do not turn aside from the point, but if I am guilty at all on this point, it is rather in being too silent than in saying too much. My purpose here is not to amuse your curiosity by novelty of the subject or to pretend that I have the true key of the prophecies that are as yet unfulfilled. I have never felt it justifiable for me to spend my time upon prophetic studies for which I have not the necessary talent, nor is it the vocation to which my Master has ordained me. I think some ministers would do far more for the profit of God's people if they would preach more about the first advent and less about the second. But I have chosen this topic because I believe it has practical bearings and may be made useful, instructive, and inspirational to us all."

The last sentence rings so true of the great pastoral heart of Charles Spurgeon. While he looked at the book of Revelation and the doctrine of the second coming of Christ as containing many mysteries of which no two biblical teachers seemed to agree upon, Spurgeon did not put aside the teaching as irrelevant. Rather, he looked for those aspects of the teaching that he knew would have a practical impact upon the lives of his listeners. Listen as Spurgeon explains it in his own words:

"Despite innumerable attempts by innumerable teachers to form a consistent scheme of biblical prophecy as to the future, Scripture is generally very indistinct in arrangement. There are in the Word of God many clear testimonies as to distinct events in the future, but these cannot easily be arranged in order so as to harmonize with other events; neither will the most accurate scholar, as I believe, ever make a consistent series of them so as to map them down. They are perfectly consistent, and their order is divine, but I believe that we shall need the actual fulfillment to make the plan clear. So intricate is the architecture of future history that the Architect Himself alone knows where this stone and that and the other are ordained to stand. It is not for us to fling any of the stones away or criticize it as poorly stated.

"We are only children, and our little plans of housebuilding, like children with their toy bricks, are very simple and elementary indeed. But God's architecture is of a high class, and we cannot, therefore, speculate where this event will come in or where that marvel will find its place. However, we may rest quite assured that each ordained event will follow in an orderly manner upon the other; and instead of puzzling our brains over projects of interpretation, we may be quite satisfied to take each of the facts separately as we find them, believingly expect them, and, above all, deduce from them their legitimate practical conclusions. The right way of knowing anything is to know how to act in consequence of it, and in spiritual things a man knows nothing until he lives what he knows. If you and I know the truths with regard to the future, each one as we find them in Scripture, and then act according to the inferences fairly to be drawn from them, we shall be wiser men than if we became inventors of elaborate schemes."

I invite you to read these twelve select chapters as you would listen to a trusted and skilled pastor, for that is exactly what Spurgeon was in his day. There is nothing speculative about Spurgeon's teaching; just the rocksolid truth. Spurgeon will meet you where you live, and you will not be disappointed.

Careful editing has helped to sharpen the focus of these sermons while retaining the authentic and timeless flavor they undoubtedly bring.

Behold, he cometh!" Have you and I ever realized the coming of Christ so fully as this? If we believe that the Lord Jesus has come the first time, we believe also that He will come the second time; but are these equally assured truths to us? Perhaps we have vividly realized the first appearing: from Bethlehem to Golgotha, and from Calvary to Olivet, we have traced the Lord, understanding that blessed cry, "Behold the Lamb of God, which taketh away the sin of the world" (John 1:29). Yes, the Word was made flesh and dwelt among us, and we beheld His glory, the glory as of the only begotten of the Father, full of grace and truth. But have we with equal firmness grasped the thought that He comes again? It should be to us not only a prophecy assuredly believed among us but also a scene pictured in our souls and anticipated in our hearts. My imagination has often set forth that dread scene, but better still, my faith has realized it. I have heard the chariot wheels of the Lord's approach, and I have endeavored to set my house in order for His reception. I have felt the shadow of that great cloud that shall attend Him, chilling the fervency of my worldliness. I hear even now in spirit the sound of the last trumpet, whose tremendous blast startles my soul to serious action and puts force into my life. Would God that I lived more completely under the influence of that august event! To this realization I invite you, for the benefit of a more vivid realization would be incalculable.

Chapter One

"He Cometh With Clouds"

Behold, he cometh with clouds; and every eye shall see him, and they also which pierced him: and all kindreds of the earth shall wail because of him. Even so, Amen—Revelation 1:7.

IN READING REVELATION 1, we observe that the beloved John saluted the seven churches in Asia with, "Grace be unto you, and peace" (vs. 4). Blessed men scatter blessings. When the *benediction* of God rests on us, we pour out benediction upon others. From the benediction, John's gracious heart rose into *adoration* of the great King of saints. As one of our hymns puts it, "The holy to the holiest leads." Those who are good at blessing men will be quick at blessing God.

It is a wonderful doxology that John has given us: "Unto him that loved us, and washed us from our sins in his own blood, and hath made us kings and priests unto God and his Father; to him be glory and dominion for ever and ever. Amen" (vv. 5–6). I like the Revised Version for its alliteration in this case, although I cannot prefer it for other reasons. It runs thus: "Unto him that *loveth* us, and *loosed* us from our sins by his blood." Truly our Redeemer has loosed us from sin, but the mention of His blood suggests washing rather than loosing. We can keep the alliteration and yet retain the meaning of cleansing if we read the passage, "Unto him that loved us, and laved us." *Loved* us and *laved* us. Carry those two words with you. Let them lie upon your tongue to sweeten your breath for prayer and praise. "Unto him that loved us, and laved us, be glory and dominion for ever and ever."

Then John tells of the dignity that the Lord has put upon us in making us kings and priests, and from this he ascribes royalty and dominion to the Lord Himself. John had been extolling the Great King, whom he calls the "prince of the kings of the earth" (vs. 5). Such indeed Jesus was and is and is to be. When John had touched upon that royalty that is natural to our divine Lord and that dominion that has come to Him by conquest and by the gift of the Father as the reward of all His travail, he then went on to note that He has "made us kings." Our Lord's royalty He diffuses among His redeemed. We praise Him first because He is in Himself a king and next because He is a King maker, the Fountain of honor and majesty. Jesus not only has enough of royalty for Himself but also hands a measure of His dignity to His people. He makes kings out of such common stuff as He finds in us poor sinners. Shall we not adore Him for this? Shall we not cast our crowns at His feet? He gave our crowns to us; shall we not give them to Him? "To him be glory and dominion for ever and ever. Amen" (vs. 6). King by Your divine nature! King by filial right! King maker, lifting up the beggar from the dunghill to set him among princes! King of kings by the unanimous love of all Your crowned ones! You are He whom Your brethren shall praise! Reign forever and ever! Unto You be hosannas of welcome and hallelujahs of praise. Lord of the earth and heaven, let all things that be or ever shall be render to You all glory in the highest degree.

Do not your souls take fire as you think of the praises of Emmanuel? Gladly would I fill the universe with His praise. Oh, for a thousand tongues to sing the glories of the Lord Jesus! If the Spirit who dictated the words of John has taken possession of our spirits, we shall find adoration to be our highest delight. Never are we so near to heaven as when we are absorbed in the worship of Jesus, our Lord and God. Oh, that I could now adore Him as I shall do when, delivered from this encumbering body, my soul shall behold Him in the fullness of His glory!

It would seem from the chapter that John's adoration was increased by his *expectation* of the Lord's second coming, for he cries, "Behold, he cometh with clouds." His adoration awoke his expectation, which all the while was lying in his soul as an element of that vehement heat of reverent love that he poured forth in his doxology. "Behold, he cometh," said John, and thus he revealed one source of his reverence. This exclamation was the result of his reverence. He adored until his faith realized his Lord and became a second and nobler sight.

I think, too, that John's reverence was deepened and his adoration was rendered more fervent by his conviction of the speediness of his Lord's coming. "Behold, he cometh," or is coming. John means to assert that Jesus is even now on His way. As workers are moved to be more diligent in service when they hear their master's approach, so, doubtless, saints are quickened in their devotion when they are conscious that He whom they worship is drawing near. He has gone away to the Father for a while, and so He has left us alone in this world; but He has said, "I will come again, and receive you unto myself" (John 14:3), and we are confident that He will keep His word. Sweet is the remembrance of that loving promise. That assurance is pouring its savor into John's heart while he is adoring, and it becomes inevitable, as well as most appropriate, that John's doxology should at its close introduce him to the Lord Himself and cause him to cry out, "Behold, he cometh." Having worshiped among the pure in heart, John sees the Lord; having adored the King, he sees Him assume the judgment seat and appear in the clouds of heaven. When once we enter upon heavenly things, we know not how far we can go or how high we can climb. John who began with blessing the churches now beholds his Lord.

May the Holy Spirit help us reverently to think of the wondrous coming of our blessed Lord when He shall appear to the delight of His people and the dismay of the ungodly!

I want to highlight three things from the text. They may seem commonplace to some of you, and indeed, they are the common places of our divine faith, and yet nothing can be of greater importance. The first is, *our Lord Jesus comes*: "Behold he cometh with clouds." The second is, *our Lord Jesus Christ's coming will be seen by all*: "Every eye shall see him, and they also which pierced him." And third, *this coming will cause great sorrow*: "All kindreds of the earth shall wail because of him."

Our Lord Jesus Christ Comes!

This announcement is thought worthy of a note of admiration. *Behold* indicated that there is something that we are to *hold* and *behold*. We now hear a voice crying, "Come and see." The Holy Spirit never uses superfluous words or redundant notes of exclamation: when He cries, "Behold!" it is because there is reason for deep and lasting attention. Will you turn away when He bids you pause and ponder, linger and look? You who have been beholding vanity, come and behold the fact that Jesus comes. You who have been beholding this and beholding that and thinking of nothing worthy of your thoughts, forget these passing sights and spectacles and for once behold a scene that has no parallel. It is not a monarch in her festivity but the King of kings in His glory. That same Jesus who went up from Olivet into heaven is coming again to earth in like manner as His disciples saw Him go up into heaven. Come and behold this great sight. If ever there was a thing in the world worth looking at, it is this. Behold and see if there was ever glory like unto His glory! Hearken to the midnight cry, "Behold, the bridegroom cometh!" It has practically to do with you. "Go ye out to meet him" (Matt. 25:6). This voice is to you. Do not carelessly turn aside, for the Lord God demands your attention: He commands you to "Behold!" Will you be blind when God bids you behold? Will you shut your eyes when your Savior cries, "Behold"? When the finger of inspiration points the way, will your eye fail to follow where it directs you?

If we read the words of our text carefully, this "Behold" shows us first that *this coming is to be vividly realized*. I think I see John. He is in the spirit, but he suddenly seems startled into a keener and more solemn attention. His mind is more awake than usual, though he was always a man of bright eyes that saw afar. We always liken John to the eagle for the height of his flight and the keenness of his vision, yet even he seems startled suddenly with a more astounding vision. He cries out, "Behold! Behold!" He has caught sight of his Lord. He says not, "He will come some day," but, "I can see Him. He is coming now." He has evidently realized the second advent. He has so conceived of the second coming of the Lord that it has become a matter of fact to him, a matter to be spoken of, and even to be written down.

"Behold, he cometh!" Have you and I ever realized the coming of Christ so fully as this? If we believe that the Lord Jesus has come the first time, we believe also that He will come the second time; but are these equally assured truths to us? Perhaps we have vividly realized the first appearing: from Bethlehem to Golgotha, and from Calvary to Olivet, we have traced the Lord, understanding that blessed cry, "Behold the Lamb of God, which taketh away the sin of the world" (John 1:29). Yes, the Word was made flesh and dwelt among us, and we beheld His glory, the glory as of the only begotten of the Father, full of grace and truth. But have we with equal firmness grasped the thought that He comes again? It should be to us not only a prophecy assuredly believed among us but also a scene pictured in our souls and anticipated in our hearts. My imagination has often set forth that dread scene, but better still, my faith has realized it. I have heard the chariot wheels of the Lord's approach, and I have endeavored to set my house in order for His reception. I have felt the shadow of that great cloud that shall attend Him, chilling the fervency of my worldliness. I hear even now in spirit the sound of the last trumpet, whose tremendous blast startles my soul to serious action and puts force into my life. Would God that I lived more completely under the influence of that august event! To this realization I invite you, for the benefit of a more vivid realization would be incalculable.

This coming is to be zealously proclaimed, for John does not merely calmly say, "He cometh," but he vigorously cries, "Behold, he cometh." Just as the herald of a king prefaces his message by a trumpet blast that calls attention, so John cries, "Behold!" It is no ordinary message that he brings, and he would not have us treat his word as a commonplace saying. He throws his heart into the announcement. He proclaims it loudly, he proclaims it solemnly, and he proclaims it with authority: "Behold, he cometh."

No truth should be more frequently proclaimed, next to the first coming of the Lord, than His second coming; and you cannot thoroughly set forth all the implications of the first advent if you forget the second. At the Lord's Supper, there is no discerning the Lord's body unless you discern His first coming; but there is no drinking into His cup to its fullness unless you hear Him say, "Until I come." You must look forward as well as backward. So it must be with all our ministries; they must look to Him on the cross and on the throne. We must vividly realize that He who has once come is coming yet again, or else our testimony will be marred and one-sided. We shall make poor work of preaching and teaching if we leave out either advent.

Next, *it is to be unquestionably asserted*. It is not, "Perhaps he will come." "Behold, he cometh" should be dogmatically asserted as an absolute certainty that has been realized by the heart of the man who proclaims it. All the prophets say that He will come. From Enoch down to the last that spoke by inspiration, they declare, "The Lord cometh with ten thousands of his saints" (Jude 14). You shall not find one who has spoken by the authority of God who does not, either directly or by implication, assert the coming of the Son of Man, when the multitudes born of woman shall be summoned to His judgment seat to receive the recompense of their deeds. All the promises are travailing with this prognostication, "Behold, he cometh." We have His own word for it, and this makes assurance doubly sure. He often assured His disciples that if He went away from them, He would come again to them, and He left us the Lord's Supper as a parting token to be observed until He comes. As often as we break bread we are reminded of the fact that though it is a most blessed ordinance, yet it is a temporary one and will cease to be celebrated when our absent Lord is once again present with us.

What is there to hinder Christ from coming? When I have studied and thought over this word, "Behold, he cometh," yes, I have said to myself, indeed He does; who shall hold Him back? His heart is with His church on earth. In the place where He fought the battle He desires to celebrate the victory. His delights are with the sons of men. All His saints are waiting for the day of His appearing, and He is waiting also. The very creation is made subject to vanity for a little while, but when the Lord shall come again, the creation itself also shall be delivered from the bondage of corruption into the glorious liberty of the children of God. We might question whether He would come a second time if He had not already come the first time, but if He came to Bethlehem, be assured that His feet shall yet stand upon Olivet. If He came to die, doubt not that He will come to reign. If He came to be despised and rejected of men, why should we doubt that He will come to be admired in all them that believe? His coming is to be unquestionably asserted.

This fact that He will come again *is to be taught as demanding our immediate interest*. "Behold, he cometh with clouds." Behold, look at it; meditate on it. It is worth thinking of, for it concerns you. Study it again and again. He will so soon be here that it is put in the present tense: "He cometh." That shaking of the earth, that blotting out of sun and moon, that fleeing of heaven and earth before His face—all these are so nearly here that John describes them as accomplished. "Behold, he cometh."

There is also this sense lying in the background that *He is already on the way*. All that He is doing in providence and grace is a preparation for His coming. All the events of human history, all the great decisions of His august majesty whereby He rules all things—all these are tending toward the day of His appearing. Do not think that He delays His coming and then suddenly He will return in great haste. He has arranged for it to take place as soon as wisdom allows. We know not what may make the present delay imperative, but the Lord knows, and that suffices. You grow uneasy because nearly two thousand years have passed since His ascension, and Jesus has not yet come; but you do not know what had to be arranged for and how far the lapse of time was absolutely necessary for the Lord's designs. Those are not small matters that have filled up the great pause: the intervening centuries have teemed with wonders. A thousand things may have been necessary in heaven itself before the consummation of all things could be arrived at. When our Lord comes, it shall be seen that He came as quickly as He could, speaking after the manner of His infinite wisdom, for He can only behave Himself wisely, perfectly, divinely. He cannot be moved by fear or passion so as to act hastily as you and I too often do. He dwells in the leisure of eternity and in the serenity of omnipotence. He does not have to measure out days and months and years and to accomplish so much in such a space or else leave His lifework undone; but according to the power of an endless life, He proceeds steadily on, and to Him a thousand years are but as one day. Therefore be assured that the Lord is even now coming. He is making all things work toward that grand climax. At this moment, and every moment since He went away, the Lord Jesus has been coming back again. "Behold, he cometh!" He is on the way! He is nearer every hour!

And we are told that *His coming will be attended by a peculiar sign*. "Behold, he cometh *with clouds*." We shall have no need to question whether it is the Son of Man who has come or whether He is indeed come. This is to be no secret matter: His coming will be as manifest as the clouds. In the wilderness, the presence of Jehovah was known by a visible pillar of cloud by day and an equally visible pillar of fire by night. That pillar of cloud was the sure token that the Lord was in His holy place, dwelling between the cherubim. Such is the token of the coming of the Lord Christ. "And then shall appear the sign of the Son of man in heaven: and then shall all the tribes of the earth mourn, and they shall see the Son of man coming in the clouds of heaven with power and great glory" (Matt. 24:30).

I cannot quote all the numerous passages of Scripture in which it is indicated that our Lord will come either sitting upon a cloud or "with the clouds" or "with the clouds of heaven," but such expressions are abundant. Is it not to show that His coming will be *majestic*? He makes the clouds His chariots. He comes with hosts of attendants, and these of a nobler sort than earthly monarchs can summon to do them homage. With clouds of angels, cherubim and seraphim, and all the armies of heaven, He comes. With all the forces of nature, thundercloud and blackness of tempest, the Lord of all makes His triumphant entrance to judge the world. The clouds are the dust of His feet in that dread day of battle when He shall alleviate Himself of His adversaries, shaking them out of the earth with His thunder and consuming them with the devouring flame of His lightning. All heaven shall gather with its utmost pomp to the great appearing of the Lord, and all the terrible grandeur of nature shall then be seen at its full. Not as the Man of sorrows, despised and rejected of men, shall Jesus come; but as Jehovah came upon Sinai in the midst of thick clouds and a terrible darkness, so shall He come, whose coming shall be the final judgment.

The clouds are meant to set forth the *might*, as well as the majesty, of His coming. "Ascribe ye strength unto God: his excellency is over Israel, and his strength is in the clouds" (Ps. 68:34). This was the royal token given by Daniel the prophet in his seventh chapter, the thirteenth verse, "I saw in the night visions, and, behold, one like the Son of man came with the clouds of heaven." Not less than divine is the glory of the Son of God, who once had nowhere to lay His head. The sublimest objects in nature shall most fitly minister to the manifest glory of the returning King of men. "Behold, he cometh," not with the swaddling clothes of His infancy, the weariness of His manhood, the shame of His death, but with all the glorious tapestry of heaven's high chambers. The hanging of the divine throne room shall aid His state.

The clouds also denote *the terror of His coming to the ungodly*. His saints shall be caught up together with Him in the clouds to meet the Lord in the air; but to those who shall remain on earth, the clouds shall turn their blackness and horror of darkness. Then shall the impenitent behold this dread vision—the Son of Man coming in the clouds of heaven. The clouds shall fill them with dread, and the dread shall be abundantly justified, for those clouds are big with vengeance and shall burst in judgment on their heads. His great white throne, though it is bright and lustrous with hope to His people, will with its very brightness and whiteness of immaculate justice strike dead the hopes of all those who trusted that they might live in sin and yet go unpunished.

I am in grateful circumstances because this theme requires no effort of imagination from me. To indulge fantasy on such a theme would be a wretched profanation of so sublime a subject that in its own simplicity should come home to all hearts. Think clearly for a moment till the meaning becomes real to you. Jesus Christ is coming, coming in unrivaled splendor. When He comes, He will be enthroned far above the attacks of His enemies, the persecutions of the godless, and the sneers of skeptics. He is coming in the clouds of heaven, and we shall be among the witnesses of His appearing. Let us dwell upon this truth.

Our Lord's Coming Will Be Seen by All

"Behold, he cometh with clouds, *and every eye shall see him, and they also which pierced him.*"

I gather from this expression, first, that *it will be a literal appearing and an actual sight.* If the second advent were to be a spiritual manifestation to be perceived by the minds of men, the phraseology would be, "Every mind shall perceive him." But it is not so: we read, "Every eye shall see him." Now, the mind can behold the spiritual, but the eye can see only that which is distinctly material and visible. The Lord Jesus Christ will not come spiritually, for in that sense He is always here; but He will come really and substantially, for every eye shall see Him, even those unspiritual eyes that gazed on Him with hate and pierced Him. Do not destroy the teaching of the Holy Ghost by the idea that there will be a spiritual manifestation of the Christ of God but that a literal appearing is out of the question. That would be altering the record. The Lord Jesus shall come to earth a second time as literally as He has come a first time. The same Christ who ate a piece of a broiled fish after He had risen from the dead, the same who said, "Handle me, and see; for a spirit hath not flesh and bones, as ye see me have" (Luke 24:39), this same Jesus is to come in the clouds of heaven. In the same manner as He went up He shall come down. He shall be literally seen. The words cannot be honestly read in any other way.

"Every eye shall see him." Yes, I do literally expect to see my Lord Jesus with these eyes of mine, even as that saint expected who long ago fell asleep believing that though the worms devoured his body, in his flesh he should see God, whom his eyes should see for himself, and not another (Job 19:26). There will be a real resurrection of the body, though modern man doubts it, such a resurrection that we shall see Jesus with our own eyes. We shall not find ourselves in a shadowy, dreamy land of floating fictions where we may perceive but cannot see. We shall not be airy nothings, mysterious, vague, impalpable; but we shall literally see our glorious Lord, whose appearing will be no phantom show or shadow dance. Never a day more real than the day of judgment, never a sight more true than the Son of Man upon the throne of His glory. Will you take this statement into your heart that you may feel the force of it?

Note well that *Jesus is to be seen of all kinds of living men*: every eye shall see Him—the king and the peasant, the most learned and the most ignorant. Those who were blind before shall see when He appears. I remember a man born blind who loved our Lord most intensely, and he was known to glory in this, that his eyes had been reserved for his Lord. Said he, "The first whom I shall ever see will be the Lord Jesus Christ. The first sight that greets my newly opened eyes will be the Son of Man in His glory." There is great comfort in this that we shall see the King in His beauty. Small pleasure is this to eyes that are full of filthiness and pride: you care not for this sight, and yet you must see it whether you please or do not please. You have shut your eyes to good things, but when Jesus comes you *must* see Him. All who dwell upon the face of the earth, if not at the same moment, yet with the same certainty, shall behold the once crucified Lord. They will not be able to hide themselves, nor to hide Him from their eyes. They will dread the sight, but it will come upon them, even as the sun shines on the thief who delights in the darkness. They will be obliged to own in dismay that they behold the Son of Man: they will be so overwhelmed with the sight that there will be no denying it.

He will be seen of those who have been long since dead. What a sight that will be for Judas and for Pilate and for Caiaphas and for Herod! What a sight it will be for those who, in their lifetime, said that there was no Savior and no need of one, or that Jesus was a mere man, and that His blood was not a propitiation for sin! Those who scoffed and reviled Him have long since died, but they shall all rise again and rise to this heritage among the rest—that they shall see Him whom they blasphemed sitting in the clouds of heaven. Death cannot hide you, nor the vault conceal you, nor rottenness and corruption deliver you. You are bound to see in your body the Lord who will judge both you and your fellows.

It is mentioned here that *He will especially be seen by those who pierced Him*. In this is included all the company that nailed Him to the tree, with those who took the spear and made the gash in His side, indeed, all who had a hand in His cruel crucifixion. It includes all of these, but it comprehends many more besides. "They also who pierced him" are by no means a few. Who have pierced Him? Why, those who once professed to love Him and have gone back to the world. Those who once ran well, "who did hinder you that ye should not obey the truth?" (Gal. 5:7). And now they use their tongues to speak against the Christ whom once they professed to love. They also have pierced Him whose inconsistent lives have brought dishonor upon the sacred name of Jesus. They also have pierced Him who refused His love, stifled their consciences, and refused His rebukes. They went every Sunday to hear of Him and remained hearers only, destroying their own souls rather than yield to His infinite love: these pierced His tender heart. Remember, if you persevere in piercing Him and fighting against Him, you will still have to see Him in that day, to your terror and despair.

We never know how soon we may be cut off, and then we are gone forever from the opportunity of benefiting our fellow men. It is a pity to be taken away with one opportunity of doing good undone. So would I earnestly plead with you under the shadow of this great truth: I would urge you to be ready, since we shall both behold the Lord in the day of His appearing. Yes, I shall stand in that great throng. You also will be there. How will you feel? You will not be able to excuse yourself from the gathering of that day. You will be there, one in that great multitude; and you will see Jesus the Lord as truly as if you were the only person before Him, and He will look upon you as certainly as if you were the only one that was summoned to His judgment seat.

Will you kindly think of all this as I close this second point? Silently repeat to yourself the words, "Every eye shall see him, and they also that pierced him."

His Coming Will Be With Great Sorrow

What does the text say about His coming? "All kindreds of the earth shall wail because of him."

"All kindreds of the earth." Then *this sorrow will be very general*. You thought, perhaps, that when Christ came, He would come to a glad world, welcoming Him with song and music. You thought that there might be a few ungodly persons who would be destroyed with the breath of His mouth, but that the bulk of mankind would receive Him with delight. See how different—"All kindreds of the earth," that is, all sorts of men that belong to the earth, all earth-born men, men out of all nations and kindreds and tongues shall weep and wail and gnash their teeth at His coming. This is a sad outlook! We have no smooth things to prophesy. What do you think of this?

Next, *this sorrow will be very great*. They shall *wail*. I cannot put into English the full meaning of that most expressive word. Sound it at length, and it conveys its own meaning. It is as when men wring their hands and burst out into a loud cry, or as when Eastern women in their anguish rend their garments and lift up their voices with the most mournful notes. All the "kindreds of the earth shall wail": wail as a mother laments over her dead child, wail as a man might wail who found himself hopelessly imprisoned and doomed to die. Such will be the hopeless grief of all the kindreds of the earth at the sight of Christ in the clouds: if they remain impenitent, they shall not be able to be silent; they shall not be able to repress or conceal their anguish, but they shall wail to their horror. What a sound that will be that will go up before high heaven when Jesus sits upon the cloud and in the fullness of His power summons them to judgment!

Will your voice be heard in that wailing? Will your heart be breaking in that general dismay? How will you escape? Unless you now fly to Christ and hide yourself in Him, and so become one of the kindred of heaven, one of His chosen and blood-washed ones—who shall praise His name for washing them from their sins—unless you do this, there will be wailing at the judgment seat of Christ, and you will be in it.

Then it is quite clear that men will not be universally converted when Christ comes, because if they were so, they would not wail. Then they would lift up the cry, "Welcome, welcome, Son of God!" These acclamations come from His people. But according to the text, the multitude of mankind will weep and wail, and therefore they will not be among His people. Do not, therefore, look for salvation to some coming day, but believe in Jesus now, and find in Him your Savior at once. If you joy in Him now, you shall much more rejoice in Him in that day; but if you will have cause to wail at His coming, it will be well to wail at once.

Note one more truth. It is quite certain that when Jesus comes in those latter days, *men will not be expecting great things of Him.* Today some teachers deceive their people with the idle dream of repentance and restoration after death, a fiction unsupported by the least tittle of Scripture. If these "kindreds of the earth" expected that when Christ would come they would all die out and cease to be, they would rejoice that thereby they escaped the wrath of God. If they thought that at His coming there would be a universal restoration and a general deliverance of souls long shut up in prison, would they wail? If Jesus could be supposed to come to proclaim a general restoration, they would not wail but would shout for joy. Ah, no! It is because His coming to the impenitent is black with blank despair that they will wail because of Him. If His first coming does not give you eternal life, His second coming will not. If you do not hide in His wounds when He comes as your Savior, there will be no hiding place for you when He comes as your Judge. They will weep and wail because, having rejected the Lord Jesus, they have turned their backs on the last possibility of hope.

Why do they wail *because of Him?* Will it not be because they will see Him in His glory and will recall that they slighted and despised Him? They will see Him come to judge them, and they will remember that once He stood at their door with mercy in His hands and said, "Open to Me," but they would not admit Him. They refused His blood; they refused His righteousness; they scoffed at His sacred name; and now they must give an account for this wickedness. They put Him away in scorn, and now, when He comes, they have solemnly to give Him their life's account. See, the books are opened! They are covered with dismay as they remember their sins and know that they are written down by a faithful pen. They must give an account, and unwashed and unforgiven they cannot render that account without knowing that the sentence will be, "Depart, ye cursed." This is why they weep and wail because of Him.

O reader, my natural love of ease makes me wish that I could preach pleasant things to you, but they are not in my commission. I dare not preach a soft gospel. As I love your immortal soul, I dare not flatter you. As I shall have to answer for it in the last great day, I must tell you the truth. Seek the mercy of God now. I have come to implore you to be reconciled to God. "Kiss the Son, lest he be angry, and ye perish from the way, when his wrath is kindled but a little. Blessed are all they that put their trust in him" (Ps. 2:12).

But if you will not have my Lord Jesus, He comes all the same for that. He is on the road now, and when He comes, you will wail because of Him. Oh, that you would make Him your friend and then meet Him with joy! Why will you die? He gives life to all those who trust Him. Believe and live.

The King is on His way and almost here. You are at His door; He is at yours. What manner of people should you be? How can you sin against One who is so close at hand? How can you rebel against One whose eyes of fire behold and whose hand of vengeance is uplifted to smite the sinner? The words of the text are very forcible. The apostle says, "What manner of persons ought ye to be?" Remember he was talking to saints, and he teaches us that even saints should be more saintly than they are. He is not saying to the ungodly, "What manner of persons ought ye to be?" He might have spoken this way; but with how much greater force does he address those who profess to be loved with the everlasting love of God, to have been bought with the precious blood of Jesus, to be pledged to Christ in eternal wedlock, to be members of His body, parts of Himself. "What manner of persons ought ye to be?" He implies that they are not what they should be, and I am afraid there is no man of God but what will grant the truth of the implication in his own case. We have not attained to what we should be, and I may say to the best child of God, "Dear brother, there is a yet beyond." Ay, brethren, and the text is so broad in its expression that it plainly teaches the limitless nature of Christian holiness. "What manner of persons ought ye to be!" as if he could not tell what sort of persons they should be: as if holiness had in it no Ultima Thule, no pillars of Hercules beyond which the adventurous mariner might not go. There is a yet beyond for us all. If we are to be holy as God is, His is infinite holiness, and where can a limit be imagined?

Chapter Two

The World on Fire

But the day of the Lord will come as a thief in the night; in the which the heavens shall pass away with a great noise, and the elements shall melt with fervent heat, the earth also and the works that are therein shall be burned up. Seeing then that all these things shall be dissolved, what manner of persons ought ye to be in all holy conversation and godliness—2 Peter 3:10–11.

PEOPLE HAVE FREQUENTLY INFERRED liberty to sin from the apparent absence of God's presence in the world. Because the Lord, in His infinite long-suffering, has allowed sin to go unpunished for a while, they have wickedly said, "How does God know? The Almighty is not even aware of us. He will interfere neither to punish men nor to reward them, whether they break or keep His commandments." When a long time occurs where there is no great change in the world, no remarkable judgment, no visitation of famine, pestilence, or war, men are very apt to take license to sin from the merciful reprieve that should have led them to gratitude, and through gratitude to obedience.

At certain periods of history it has seemed to the Most High to be imperatively necessary to send great calamities upon mankind lest pride, oppression, and profanity should cause society utterly to rot. The fall of dynasties, the overthrow of empires, devastating wars, and dire famines have been necessities of God's moral government—bits in men's mouths, bridles for their arrogance, checks to their licentiousness. The Lord is slow to judge the wicked, for

27

His tender mercy is great, and He does not delight in the sufferings of men; and therefore He keeps His arrows in His quiver and hangs up His bow. But, alas, men take advantage of His love to grow grossly sinful and to blaspheme His name.

Against this spirit the apostle Peter is arguing in this chapter. The profanely secure had said, "Where is the promise of his coming? for since the fathers fell asleep, all things continue as they were" (2 Pet. 3:4). They say, "Where is the evidence of God's existence? The world goes on like a clock, needing no hand to move its wheels or guide its action. There is no God to interfere, and we may live as we want." "No," says Peter, "but God has interfered." And though he might have quoted a thousand other instances, Peter preferred to put his finger upon the great event of Noah's flood and say, "Here at least God did interfere." God could no longer bear the transgressions of mankind, and therefore He pulled up the sluices of the great deep and opened the floodgates of heaven. He commanded the angry floods to leap forth from their lairs, and they swallowed up the earth. So, says Peter, it is plain that things have not all continued in one course; there have been interventions of divine justice. The apostle then tells the scoffer that there will be another intervention before long, but instead of water, fire shall be the instrument of destruction. God's mill grinds slowly, but it grinds to powder. Justice may linger to commune with mercy, but it rapidly makes up for its delay. Long is the blow withheld, but when it falls it cuts to the soul. God's wrath is long in kindling, but in the end it shall burn as an oven.

The Last Judgment

Despite innumerable attempts by innumerable teachers to form a consistent scheme of biblical prophecy as to the future, Scripture is generally very indistinct in arrangement. There are in the Word of God many clear testimonies as to distinct events in the future, but these cannot easily be arranged in order so as to harmonize with other events; neither will the most accurate scholar, as I believe, ever make a consistent series of them so as to map them down. They are perfectly consistent, and their order is divine, but I believe that we shall need the actual fulfillment to make the plan clear. So intricate is the architecture of future history that the Architect Himself alone knows where this stone and that and the other are ordained to stand. It is not for us to fling any of the stones away or criticize it as poorly stated.

We are only children, and our little plans of housebuilding, like children with their toy bricks, are very simple and elementary indeed. But God's architecture is of a high class, and we cannot, therefore, speculate where this event will come in or where that marvel will find its place. However, we may rest quite assured that each ordained event will follow in an orderly manner upon the other; and instead of puzzling our brains over projects of interpretation, we may be quite satisfied to take each of the facts separately as we find them, believingly expect them, and, above all, deduce from them their legitimate practical conclusions. The right way of knowing anything is to know how to act in consequence of it, and in spiritual things a man knows nothing until he lives what he knows. If you and I know the truths with regard to the future, each one as we find them in Scripture, and then act according to the inferences fairly to be drawn from them, we shall be wiser men than if we became inventors of elaborate schemes.

In Peter's second epistle, there is one truth very plainly taught—namely, that this present world is to be consumed by fire. We learn also that this fire will take place in connection with the judgment, for "the heavens and the earth, which are now, by the same word are kept in store, reserved unto fire against the day of judgment and perdition of ungodly men" (2 Pet. 3:7). The former destruction of the world by a flood of water was in consequence of sin and was a declaration of God's wrath against it; it did not happen as an accident or occur without design. Man sinned, was warned, and sinned again, until God saw that the wickedness of man was great in the earth. Finally, the Lord's spirit was so grieved that He would no longer strive with man. Floods of sin called for floods of destruction.

So it will be with the last fire; it will happen not as an inevitable result of physical causes but because God intends to purge this material world from all traces of sin. The world has been defiled, and before He makes it into a new heaven and a new earth, He will cleanse it as by fire. Under the Levitical dispensation, the cleansing of vessels that had been defiled was effected by passing them through the fire, as a type of the intense energy needed to remove sin and the Lord's abhorrence of it; so shall this earth dissolve with fervent heat, and thus the Lord shall proclaim to the whole universe that He hates even the garment spotted by the flesh. When a house was defiled with leprosy, it was destroyed, and so must this earth be, for the plague of sin has polluted it.

We gather also from our text that this fire will burn up all the works existing upon the earth—everything that man has constructed shall perish. We have heard architects speak of buildings that will stand up to anything! Aha! They have been built but for an hour, and their noblest fabrics will disappear like children's castles of sand upon the sea beach. Down will go the vast cathedrals and the towering palaces in one common crash; whole cities will flame upon earth's funeral pyre, while forests and melting mountains blend their smoke. The pride of power, the pomp of wealth, the beauty of art, the cunning of skill—all, all, must go. The sea of flame will overwhelm and devour everything without exception. The massive masonry and rocklike foundations of our vast engineering works shall run like wax in the tremendous heat. So fierce will be the flames that everything capable of being burned will be utterly consumed, and the elements, or the solid portions of the earth, shall be liquefied by the intense heat. Rocks, metals, everything shall dissolve, and the atmosphere itself shall burn with fury when its oxygen shall unite with the hydrogen and other gases liberated by the intense heat. Chemists tell us that the great noise that Peter speaks of would certainly accompany such a combustion. The whole world shall become one molten mass again, and this terrestrial firmament shall cease to be. "The heavens shall vanish away like smoke, and the earth shall wax old like a garment" (Isa. 51:6). God has impressed nature with His seal today, but He will melt it down and then, as we hope, will pour out the molten matter and stamp upon it a yet more lovely image than it has ever borne before.

We may here note that the prophecy that the earth will thus be consumed with fervent heat is easy to believe not only because God says it but also because there are evidently the means at hand for the accomplishment of the prophecy. The Roman writer Pliny was known to say that it was a miracle that the world escaped burning for a single day, and I do not wonder at the remark, considering the character of the region in which he spent much of his time. In visiting the country around Naples, the same thought constantly occurred to me. Vesuvius was ready at any moment to vomit fire and continually sends up clouds of smoke. Ascend the mountainside, climbing over ashes and masses of lava: all beneath you is glowing; thrust in your staff and it is charred. Then go across to the solfatara on the other side of Naples and stand at the vent of that ancient volcano and listen to the terrible rumblings that attend the rush of steam and sulfur. Then stamp your foot or dash a stone upon the ground and hear how the earth resounds; it is evident that you are standing over a vast cavern. Look around you and remark how the earth steams with sulfurous exhalations. Observe also how the earth in some places has risen and fallen, again and again. Down there at Puteoli in the Temple of Serapis are pillars that have sunk below the tide mark and then have risen above it several times, as you can see for yourself by the mark of the sea worms. In a single night, vast hills have risen in one place like bubbles upon the baker's dough, while in other localities there have been equally sudden subsidings of the surface.

Yet this volcanic region around Naples is but one of the many vent holes of the great fires that are in the depths of the earth. Hundreds more burning mountains have already vomited flames. According to the belief of many geologists, the whole center of the earth is a mass of molten matter, and we live upon a thin crust that has cooled down and is probably not so much as one hundred miles thick. Everyone who is at all acquainted with the condition of the globe knows that it needs only the Lord's will, and the fiery sea, of which the volcanoes are but the safety valve, would burst forth and flood the earth with flame, or if God so willed it, the thin crust that divides the ocean of water from the ocean of fire might soon be broken through and the result must be disruption and destruction.

But if there were no internal sea of fire, who can guess the power that lurks in other subtle forces of nature, such as electricity? What reserves of destructive force there must be in and around the globe! God's dreadful armies lie in ambush everywhere; what if I say that God's bodyguard is sleeping in His guard chamber? He has but to speak the word, and the servants of His omnipotence will rise, terrible in their destructive power. He spoke to His ancients of the sea, and they marched in gigantic might till they had covered the mountaintops and laid the race of men dead at their feet, except for Noah and his family. Let Him but speak to His ministers of flaming fire and they will at once subdue the globe by quenchless burnings. Earth is as a pile of wood, and the torchbearers stand ready to kindle it at any moment. There has always been a cry of fire among men, and the cry goes louder every century, for the burning is near.

But if there were no such arrangements as these, we should still be bound to believe what God has said. It is His solemn declaration that the day shall come when the Lord Jesus Christ shall appear as a thief in the night, and the heavens, that is the atmosphere, shall pass away with a great noise, while the elements, or rudimentary substances of the globe, shall melt with fervent heat. The earth also, and the works that are therein, or thereon, shall be burned up.

We gather from our text that this will happen at a time when it will not be expected. The dread hour will come as a thief in the night. It was not expected in Noah's day that the world would be destroyed. That was not for any lack of warning but because men could not imagine it possible. They argued against Noah that all things had continued as they were from the days of their first father, Adam, and that so they would be. They thought Noah a fool for going up and down the world proclaiming an absurdity and frightening people with a fairy tale.

They respond the same today when God's Word declares that the whole world will be destroyed by fire. They reject the testimony and continue in sin, in worldliness, and in rebellion against God; and so will they do up to the very moment when the shrill sound of the trump shall convince them that the Lord has come and that the day of judgment and damnation of ungodly men has arrived. No preaching will of itself avail to make ungodly men expect the coming of Christ, however clear, bold, consistent, and long contin-ued it may be. The world is obsessed with its idols, its ear is too dull to hear the truth; we will never charm this cobra into listening to warning. Men's eyes are blinded, they will not see, and so they hurry on to their doom, and then "when they shall say, Peace and safety; then sudden destruction cometh upon them, as travail upon a woman with child; and they shall not escape" (1 Thess. 5:3).

We should remind ourselves again that the long time that has intervened since Peter foretold the destruction of the world by fire is to be understood in the sense of infinite mercy. We are not to interpret it according to the wicked suggestion of unbelief, for the Lord will surely be revealed in flaming fire. We are to read it with the eyes of faith and gratitude. God waits that men may be saved. He delays that in this long time of waiting, hundreds everywhere may believe in Jesus and enter into eternal life, and while we may consistently desire to hasten the coming of the Lord, we may be equally content that mercy's day should be lengthened. While I have prayed "Come quickly," I have often felt inclined to contradict myself and cry, "Yet wait for a while, good Lord: let mercy's day be lengthened, let the heathen yet receive the Savior." We may desire the coming of the Lord, but we should also be in sympathy with the Most High's patience, to which His loving heart inclines Him.

Although we read of the world being burned with fire, we are not told that it will be annihilated. We know that nothing has been annihilated yet. No fire has yet been able to destroy a single atom of matter. There is upon the face of the earth at this moment just as much matter as when God created it: fire changes form but does not obliterate substance. This world, so far as we know, will not cease to be; it will pass through the purifying flame, and then it may be the soft and gentle breath of Almighty love will blow upon it and cool it rapidly, and the divine hand will shape it as it cools into a paradise more fair than that which bloomed upon the banks of Hiddekel. We believe from various Scriptures, though we would not dogmatize, that this world will be refitted and renovated; and in that sense we expect new heavens and a new earth, wherein dwells righteousness. Martin Luther used to say that the world is now in its working clothes and that the day would come when it will be arrayed in its Easter garments of joy.

One likes to think that the trail of the old serpent will not always remain upon the globe, and it is a cheering thought that where sin has abounded, God's glory should yet more abound. I cannot believe that the world where Jesus was born and lived and died will be annihilated. Surely an earth with a Calvary upon it must last on. Will not the blood of Jesus immortalize it? It has groaned and travailed with mankind, being made subject to vanity for our sake. Surely it is to have its joyful redemption and keep its Sabbaths after the fire has burned out every trace of sin and sorrow. Whether or not it shall be so matters little to the saints, for we shall be with Christ where He is and behold His glory; and as to the future, "forever with the Lord" may well satisfy us.

Practical Inferences

"Seeing then that all these things shall be dissolved, what manner of persons ought ye to be in all holy conversation and godliness?" What does Peter mean by this? What connection can there be between the burning of the earth and holy behavior and godliness? The first connection is this. Our position as Christians is at this moment like that of Noah before the destruction of the world by water. What manner of person should Noah have been? He said to himself, "This fair and beautiful world in which I dwell will soon be covered with the ooze and slime of a tremendous deluge." He looked upon the rest of mankind, and he thought and said of them, "Except these people fly to the ark and are sheltered with me, every one of them will be drowned." He saw them marrying and given in marriage, feasting and playing at the very hour when the flood came, and he felt that if they would believe as he did, they would find something else to do than to be engrossed in carnal pleasures. When he saw them heaping up money, he would almost laugh yet weep to think that they should hoard up gold to be submerged with themselves in the general flood. When men added to their estates acre after acre, I have no doubt the patriarch said to himself, "The flood will sweep away all these landmarks, and as it carries away the owner so will it destroy all traces of his barn and his farm and his fields." I should suppose such a man, daily expecting the rain to descend and the flood to burst up from beneath, would lead a life very free from worldliness, a life the very reverse of the rest of mankind. They would reckon Noah to be very eccentric, they would be unable to understand him, and indeed his conduct would be such that no one could understand it except upon the theory that he believed in the destruction of all around him.

Now our life should be like that of Noah. Look around on the beauties of nature, and when you enjoy them say to yourself, "All these are to be dissolved and to melt with fervent heat." Look up into the clear blue and think that the sky itself shall shrivel like a scroll and be rolled up like a garment that has seen its better days and must be put aside. Look on your neighbors, your own children, and your household, and those you pass in the street or meet with in transacting business, and say, "Alas, alas, unless these men, women, and children fly to Jesus and are saved in Him, they will be destroyed with the earth on which they dwell, for the day of the Lord is surely coming, and judgment awaits the ungodly." This should make us act in a spirit that is the opposite of those who now say, "Let us buy and sell and get gain, let us heap together treasure, let us live for this world, let us eat and drink and be merry." They are of the earth; therefore their conduct and conversation are earthy. As there is down deep in your heart an object different from theirs, and as you set a different estimate on all things, your conduct will be very distinct from theirs. Being swayed by different motives, your life will diverge from theirs, and they will misunderstand you, and while trying to find motives for you, as they do not know the true motive, they will impute unfavorable motives to you. But so it must be. You must come out from among them, be separate and touch not the unclean thing; and the fact that all these things are to be burnt up should make it easy for you to do so, nay, natural for you to do so, as it must have made it both easy and natural to the patriarch Noah.

I will not, however, dwell longer upon that thought but will remark further that the nearness of the Lord as suggested by the fact that the world is to be destroyed, according to His word, suggests holiness. The sinner finds a reason for sin when he says, "God is not here, and therefore everything goes on in the ordinary way. God does not care what men do." "No," says the apostle Peter. "He is not away. He is here, holding back the fire forces. He is reserving this world a little while, and by and by He will let the fires loose and the world will be destroyed. He is not far off: He is even at the door." If I give the Greek rendering, it should be, "All these things are dissolving." They are even now beginning to dissolve; they are in the process of dissolution. God is close upon us; can you not hear His footfall? Christ is returning; He is on His journey now. Faith hears the tramp of His steeds as they hurry on the chariot of His vengeance. "Behold, I come quickly" is the word that rings over the mountains of division. The King is coming; He is coming to His throne and to His judgment. A man does not go up to a king's door and there talk treason, and men do not sit in a king's chamber when they expect him at every moment to enter and there speak ill of him.

The King is on His way and almost here. You are at His door; He is at yours. What manner of people should you be? How can you sin against One who is so close at hand? How can you rebel against One whose eyes of fire behold and whose hand of vengeance is uplifted to smite the sinner? The words of the text are very forcible. The apostle says, "What manner of persons ought ye to be?" Remember he was talking to saints, and he teaches us that even saints should be more saintly than they are. He is not saying to the ungodly, "What manner of persons ought ye to be?" He might have spoken this way; but with how much greater force does he address those who profess to be loved with the everlasting love of God, to have been bought with the precious blood of Jesus, to be pledged to Christ in eternal wedlock, to be members of His body, parts of Himself. "What manner of persons ought ye to be?" He implies that they are not what they should be, and I am afraid there is no man of God but what will grant the truth of the implication in his own case. We have not attained to what we should be, and I may say to the best child of God, "Dear brother, there is a yet beyond." Ay, brethren, and the text is so broad in its expression that it plainly teaches the limitless nature of Christian holiness. "What manner of persons ought ye to be!" as if he could not tell what sort of persons they should be: as if holiness had in it no *Ultima Thule*, no pillars of Hercules beyond which the adventurous mariner might not go. There is a yet beyond for us all. If we are to be holy as God is, His is infinite holiness, and where can a limit be imagined?

And then Peter goes on to specify two branches of holy life. "In all holy conversation," that is to say, all holy behavior toward men, "and godliness," that is, all pious dealing toward God. True religion by no means depreciates the duties of the second table of the law. Some professing believers think very little of the common virtues of daily life, but they err greatly and will find themselves in an evil predicament at last. If the grace you possess does not make you honest, God have mercy on you and take such grace away from you. If you have a kind of grace that does not keep you sexually pure in body and mind and make your behavior decent, if you have a sort of grace that lets you cheat and lie, that allows you to take undue advantage in business, away with such grace. That is the grace of the devil but not the grace of God, and may you be saved from it. If our religion does not make us moral, it is a millstone about our necks to destroy us. If you have not reached morality, how can you dare to talk about holiness, which is a far higher and loftier thing? The best morality in the world will not prove a man to be a Christian, but if a man does not have morality, it proves that he is not a child of God.

And then as to God: the duties of the first table of the law are not to be neglected. We are to fulfill all manner of godliness. God is to be worshiped by us devoutly, and we are to take pains to worship Him in His own way. How many people have a kind of—what shall I call it?—a happy-go-lucky religion. Whatever their mother or their father was, that are they. A great many go to certain places of worship not because they have ever inquired whether the group they belong to is right or not but because they have drifted that way, and there they stick. How few take the Bible and search for themselves, yet no man has obeyed God correctly who has not done so. If I could not honestly say, "I am a member of this denomination because I have weighed the truths that are held by my brethren, and I believe them to be according to God's book," I could not feel that I had done right toward the Most High.

The idea that there are good people in all sects is well enough, but a great many have perverted it into an excuse for never caring what God's truths or ordinances are. Rest assured that he who neglects one of the least of Christ's ordinances and teaches men so, the same shall be least in the kingdom of heaven. Every truth is important. Trivializing conscience is the sin of the present age. Men have even come to occupy pulpits in churches when they do not believe the fundamental doctrines of the Church. We have heard them even claim a right to retain their pulpits after they have denied the doctrines of the denomination to which they belong. May God deliver every one of us from a conscience that approves anything that a person desires. Be right even in little things. Be precise: you serve a precise God. Charity towards others is one thing; laxity for yourself is quite another thing.

The fleetingness of all things around us suggests our looking away to eternal things. We should live always as if we might die in a moment. John Wesley once said, "Now, if I knew I should die tomorrow morning, I would do exactly what I have planned to do. I should take the class meeting at such an hour, preach at such an hour, and be up at such a time in the morning to pray." That good man's life was spent in prospect of sudden departure, and it was therefore active and holy. Is ours the same? The motive for holiness becomes stronger still if the thought is not merely that I shall die but that all these things around me shall be dissolved. That breezy range, that towering hill, the lofty trees and this overhanging cliff, these rich meadows, the ripening harvest, all, all, will in a moment be on a blaze. Am I ready to be caught away to be with my Lord in the air? Or shall I be left to perish amidst the conflagration? How should I live! I should stand as it were on tiptoe, ready when He shall call me to be away up into the glory far off from this perishing world! It makes us look upon all these things in a different light and upon eternal things with a more fixed eye and a more stern resolve to live for God.

Observe that if sin even on the inanimate world needs such a purging by fire as this, if the fact that here sin has been committed makes it needful that God should burn it all up, what a horrid thing sin must be! Oh, to be purged from it! Refining fire, go through my heart! Spirit of the living God, sweep with all Your mighty burnings through and through my body, soul, and spirit till You have purged me of every tendency to sin. This should be the prayer of the Christian. And if, again, God is so angry with sin that when He comes to judge it He will come with flaming fire, and if the terrors of God against the wicked will be utterly overwhelming, what gratitude should you and I feel for pardoned sin, what joy for safety in the Lord Jesus Christ. And then, again, as the result of that, what a detestation of the sin that made it needful that Christ should die to save us from the wrath to come! Believer in Jesus, you will never have to escape from those tongues of flame that will lick up the sea; you will not be alarmed at the melting mountains; you will be safe; not a hair of your head shall be singed. Oh, what do you owe to sovereign grace for such an escape as this! Bless the Lord Jesus, fall down at His dear feet and adore Him, and then, rising up, say, "What can I do to glorify You? O Lord keep me clear of the sin that would have destroyed me, and help me to live such a life as is fitting for one who has been saved from the wrath to come."

Once more, Peter meant us to feel that the suddenness of all this should keep us on our watchtower. This universal fire will come with no signs to herald it that the ungodly will observe. You who are on the watch will observe them; you will see the signs of His coming; you will rejoice to go forth to meet Him. But to the ungodly, His coming will be as much unawares as was His first advent that happened in the night when all the world was wrapped in sleep. Men will still be buying and selling and getting gain and thinking of nothing so little as of the last advent, and then the Lord will appear. Christian, let not that day come upon you as a thief. Stand ever watching. Live as if you said to yourself, "Today everything I have may be burned up; today all my lands may run like lava, all my gold may melt like molten lead; today I myself may have done with this world, and the world may be consumed." Live such a life as that.

"Why," says one, "then we should be pilgrims and strangers in this world." That is just how you should be. "Then," says another, "we should not be so concerned about the money in the bank and laying up for the future." Just so. That is how the Master would have you live: He would have you appropriately prudent and provident but not covetous or anxious. If you feel that all these things are to be dissolved, you will then do all things as in the presence of God. You will wish to use everything you have as not abusing it, and as reckoning that it will perish in the using. God grant you so to live.

I would to God that every reader was prepared for the future. You remember John Bunyan makes Christian sit in the City of Destruction at ease until he hears from one called Evangelist that the city was to be burned up, and then he cries, "Alas, alas, woe is me, and I shall be destroyed in it." That thought set him running, and nothing could stop him. His wife called for him to come back, but he said, "The city is to be destroyed, and I must flee." His children clung to his garments to hold him, but he said, "No, I must run to the City of Safety, for this city is to be burned up." Man, it will all go! If all you love is here below, it will all go! Your gold and silver will all go! Will you not have Christ? Will you not have a Savior? If you will not, there remains for you only a fearful looking for of judgment and of fiery indignation. Tempt not the anger of God. Yield to His mercy now. Believe in His dear Son.

*B*ut after the resurrection, according to the text, comes the judgment. You have cursed God, but the foul word died away. No, it did not; it imprinted itself upon the great book of God's remembrance. You may have entered the chamber of pleasure or the hall of infidelity, you may have walked through the stews of crime and through the stench and filth of the sexually impure. You have wandered into sin and plunged into it, thinking that it would all die with the day, that as the night covers up the sights of the day, so the night of death should cover up the deeds of your day of life. Not so. The books shall be opened. I think I see you closing your eyes because you dare not look upon the Judge when He opens that page where your history stands. I hear the boldest of sinners crying to the sublime and dread granite rocks, "Fall on me." He would rather be crushed than stand there before the avenging eye; but the mountains will not loosen, their flinty bowels feel no pangs of sympathy, they will not move. You stand while the dread voice reads on, and on, and on, your every act and word and thought. I see you as the shameful list is read, and men and angels hear. I see your horror as a nameless deed is told, in terms explicit, that none can misunderstand. I hear your thoughts brought out—that lust, that murder that was in the thought, but never grew into the deed. And you are all this time astonished like Belshazzar, when he saw the writing on the wall and he was terribly afraid. So shall it be with you.

Chapter Three

The First Resurrection

And I saw thrones, and they sat upon them, and judgment was given unto them: and I saw the souls of them that were beheaded for the witness of Jesus, and for the word of God, and which had not worshiped the beast, neither his image, neither had received his mark upon their foreheads, or in their hands; and they lived and reigned with Christ a thousand years. But the rest of the dead lived not again until the thousand years were finished. This is the first resurrection. Blessed and holy is he that hath part in the first resurrection: on such the second death hath no power, but they shall be priests of God and of Christ, and shall reign with him a thousand years.... And I saw the dead, small and great, stand before God; and the books were opened: and another book was opened, which is the book of life: and the dead were judged out of those things which were written in the books, according to their works—Revelation 20:4–6, 12.

IT IS RARE THAT I INTRUDE into the mysteries of the future with regard to either the second coming, the millennial reign, or the first and second resurrection. As often as I come across it in my expositions, I do not turn aside from the point, but if I am guilty at all on this point, it is rather in being too silent than in saying too much. My purpose here is not to amuse your curiosity by novelty of the subject or to pretend that I have the true key of the prophecies that are as yet unfulfilled. I have never felt it justifiable for me to spend my time upon prophetic studies for which I have not the necessary talent, nor is it the vocation to which my Master has ordained me. I think some ministers would do far more for the profit of God's people if they would preach more about the first advent and less about the second. But I have chosen this topic because I believe it has practical bearings and may be made useful, instructive, and inspirational to us all.

In my studies, I find that the most sincere of the preachers among the Puritans did not hesitate to dwell upon this mysterious subject. I turn to Charnock, who in his thesis upon the immutability of God does not hesitate to speak of the judgment of the world, of the millennial reign, and of the new heavens and new earth. I turn to Richard Baxter, a man who above all other men loved the souls of men, who more perhaps than any other man, with the exception of the apostle Paul, travailed for souls; and I find him making a barbed arrow out of the doctrine of the coming of the Lord and thrusting this great truth into the very heart and conscience of unbelievers as though it were heaven's own sword. And John Bunyan, too—plain, honest John—he who preached so simply that a child could comprehend him and was certainly never guilty of having written upon his forehead the word *mystery*—he, too, speaks of the advent of Christ and of the glories that shall follow, using this doctrine as an encouragement to the saints and as a warning to the ungodly. I do not think, therefore, I need tremble very much if the charge should be brought against me of bringing before you an unprofitable subject.

The Three Privileges

"Blessed and holy is he that hath part in the first resurrection: on such the second death hath no power, but they shall be priests of God and of Christ, and shall reign with him a thousand years."

Before I proceed to enter into the privileges stated in this text, I must remark that I am aware of two modes of understanding this verse, both of which I think are untenable. One opinion holds that the first resurrection here spoken of is a *resurrection of principles*—the resurrection of the patience, the undaunted courage, the holy boldness, and the constancy of the ancient martyrs. It says that these great principles have been forgotten and, as it were, buried, and that during the spiritual reign of Christ which is to come, these great principles will have a resurrection. Now, I appeal to you, would you in reading that passage think this to be the meaning? Is it not clear, even at a glance, that this is the resurrection of *men*? And is it not a literal resurrection, too? Does our text also say, "I saw the souls of them that were beheaded for the witness of Jesus"?

Is it not written, *"The rest of the dead lived not"*? Does this mean the rest of the dead principles? The rest of the dead doctrines? You cannot so translate it. It is—we have no doubt whatever—a literal resurrection of the saints of God and not of principles or of doctrines.

A second interpretation states that blessed and holy is he who has been born again and so has had a resurrection from dead works by the resurrection of the Lord Jesus Christ. The difficulty here is how to make this metaphorical interpretation agree with the literal fact that the rest of the dead lived not till the thousand years were finished? For if the first resurrection here spoken of is a metaphorical or spiritual resurrection, then the next where it speaks of the resurrection of the dead must be spiritual and mystical and metaphorical, too. Now, no one would agree to this. The laws of biblical interpretation do not allow you to read a passage of Scripture and say, "This part is a symbol and is to be read so, and the next part is to be read literally." Surely, the Holy Spirit does not jumble metaphors and literal facts together. A symbolic book has plain indications that it is so intended, and when you come upon a literal passage in a symbolic chapter, it is always attached to a something else that is distinctly literal so that you cannot, without violence to common sense, make a symbolic meaning out of it. The fact is, in reading this passage with an unbiased judgment, having no theory to defend—and I confess I have none, for I know but very little about mysteries to come—I could not help seeing *two literal resurrections* here—one of the spirits of the just, and the other of the bodies of the wicked, one of the saints who sleep in Jesus whom God shall bring with *Him*, and another of those who live and die impenitent, who perish in their sins.

All this by way of preface to the three privileges contained in the text.

The first privilege is *the priority of resurrection*. I think Scripture is exceedingly plain and explicit upon this point. You have perhaps imagined that all men will rise at the same moment, that the trump of the archangel will break open every grave at the same instant and sound in the ear of every sleeper at the identical moment. But I do not think this is the testimony of the Word of God. I think the Word of God teaches, and teaches indisputably, that the saints shall rise first. And whether the interval of time is a thousand literal years or simply a very long period of time, I am not attempting to define. My purpose is to state that there are two resurrections, a resurrection of the just, and afterward of the unjust—a time when the saints of God shall rise, and a later time when the wicked shall rise to the resurrection of damnation.

First, look at the words of the apostle in the chapter that we use generally as a text for funerals: 1 Corinthians 15:20–24: "But now is Christ risen from the dead, and become the firstfruits of them that slept. For since by man came death, by man came also the resurrection of the dead. For as in Adam all die, even so in Christ shall all be made alive. But every man in his own order: Christ the firstfruits; afterward they that are Christ's at his coming. Then cometh the end, when he shall have delivered up the kingdom to God, even the Father; when he shall have put down all rule and all authority and power." There has been an interval of two thousand years between "Christ the firstfruits" and the "afterward they that are Christ's at his coming." Why not, then, a thousand years between that first resurrection and "the end." Here is a resurrection of those who are Christ's, and of them only. As for the wicked, one would scarce know that they would rise at all from this passage if it were not for the general statement "All shall be made alive," and even this may not be so comprehensive as at first sight it seems. It is enough for me that there is here a particular and exclusive resurrection of those who are Christ's.

Turn to another passage, which is perhaps plainer still: 1 Thessalonians 4:13–17: "But I would not have you to be ignorant, brethren, concerning them which are asleep, that ye sorrow not, even as others which have no hope. For if we believe that Jesus died and rose again, even so them also which sleep in Jesus will God bring with him. For this we say unto you by the word of the Lord, that we which are alive and remain unto the coming of the Lord shall not prevent"—or have a preference beyond—"them which are asleep. For the Lord himself shall descend from heaven with a shout, with the voice of the archangel, and with the trump of God: and the dead in Christ shall rise first: then we which are alive and remain shall be caught up together with them in the clouds, to meet the Lord in the air: and so shall we ever be with the Lord." Here is nothing said whatever about the resurrection of the wicked: it is stated only that the dead in Christ shall rise first. Our apostle is evidently speaking of a first resurrection; and since we know that a first resurrection implies a second, and since we know that the wicked dead are to rise as well as the righteous dead, we draw the inference that the wicked dead shall rise at the second resurrection, after the interval between the two resurrections shall have been accomplished.

Turn to Philippians 3:8, 10–11, and compare the two verses. "Yea doubtless, and I count all things but loss for the excellency of the knowledge of Christ Jesus my Lord: for whom I have suffered the loss of all things, and do count them but dung, that I may win Christ.... That I may know him, and the power of his resurrection, and the fellowship of his sufferings, being made conformable unto his death; if by any means I might attain unto the resurrection of the dead." What does Paul mean there? Everyone will rise, no orthodox Christian doubts that. The doctrine of a general resurrection is received by all the Christian Church. What, then, is this resurrection after which Paul was exerting himself, if by any means he might attain unto it? It could not be the general resurrection; he would attain unto that however he lived his life. It must have been some superior resurrection, of which only those shall be partakers who have known Christ and the power of His resurrection, having been made conformable unto His death. I think you cannot interpret this passage or give it any force of meaning unless you admit that there is to be a prior resurrection of the just before the resurrection of the unjust.

If you will turn to a passage in Luke 20:35–36, you will find there something that I will venture to call a clear proof of a special resurrection. The Sadducees had proposed a difficulty as to the relationship of men and women in the future state, and Jesus says, "But they which shall be accounted worthy to obtain that world, and the resurrection from the dead, neither marry, nor are given in marriage: neither can they die any more: for they are equal unto the angels; and are the children of God, being the children of the resurrection." There is clearly some *worthiness* necessary for this resurrection. Do you not perceive it? There is some distinction involved in being called the children of the resurrection. Now, again I say, you do not doubt but that all people shall rise. In that sense, then, every person would be one of the children of the resurrection; in that sense, no worthiness would be required for resurrection at all. There must be, then, a resurrection for which worthiness is needed, a resurrection that shall be a distinguished privilege, which, being obtained, shall confer upon its possessor the distinguished and honorable title of a "child of the resurrection." It seems to me that this is plain enough and can be stated beyond all dispute. In Luke 14:13–14, you have a promise made to those who, when they make a feast, do not do it with the intention of getting anything in return. "But when thou makest a feast, call the poor, the maimed, the lame, the blind: and thou shalt be blessed; for they cannot recompense thee: for thou shalt be recompensed at the resurrection of the just." I would not insist upon it that this verse proves that the just rose at a different time, but still there is to be a resurrection of the just, and on the other hand, there is to be a resurrection of the unjust; and the time of recompense for the righteous is to be the resurrection of the just, which is spoken of as being a particular period. He might just as well have said, "You shalt be recompensed at the general resurrection." There was no need to have said "at the resurrection of the just" if the two are to happen at the same time. The phrase "of the just" is superfluous in the passage unless it refers to some era distinguished and distinct from the resurrection of the unjust. I will not say that this is absolute proof, but still, all these things put together, with other passages I might quote if I had the space, would, I think, establish upon a scriptural basis the doctrine of the two resurrections.

But I would refer to one more, which seems to me to be exceedingly clear, in John 6:39, 40, 44, 54. In these verses the Savior four times over speaks of His own believing people and promises them a resurrection, "I will raise him up at the last day." Now, is there any joy or beauty in this, to the people of God in particular, unless there is something special in it for them? It is the lot of all to rise, and yet we have here a privilege for the elect! Surely, there is a different resurrection. Besides, there is yet a passage that now springs to my memory in Hebrews 11:35, speaking of the trials of the godly and their noble endurance and referring to them as, "not accepting deliverance; that they might obtain a better resurrection." The betterness was not in the later results of resurrection but in the resurrection itself. How, then, could it be a better resurrection unless there is some distinction between the resurrection of the saint and the resurrection of the sinner? Let the one be a resurrection of splendor, let the other be a resurrection of gloom and horror, and let there be a marked division between the two, that as it was in the beginning, it may be even to the end, the Lord has put a difference between him who fears God and him who fears Him not.

I now pass on to the second privilege here promised to the godly. *The second death has no power over them.* This, too, is a literal death, nonetheless literal because its main terror is spiritual, for a spiritual death is as literal as a physical death. The death that shall come upon the ungodly without exception can never touch the righteous. Oh, this is the best of all! As for the first resurrection, if Christ has granted that to His people, there must be something glorious in it if we cannot perceive it: "It doth not yet appear what we shall be: but we know that, when he shall appear, we shall be like *him*" (1 John 3:2). I think the glories of the first resurrection belong to the glories that shall be revealed *in* us rather than the glories that are revealed *to* us. What shall be the majesty of that form in which we shall rise, what the distinguished happiness we shall then enjoy, we can only guess at a distance, and we certainly cannot know it to the full. But on this point we can understand what Scripture states, that damnation, the second death, shall have no power on those who rise at the first resurrection. How should it? How can damnation fall on any but those who are sinners and are guilty of sin? But the saints are not guilty of sin. They have sinned like others, and they were by nature the children of wrath even as others. But their sin has been lifted from them: it was laid upon the eternal Substitute, even our Lord Jesus. He carried all their guilt and their iniquity into the wilderness of forgetfulness, where it shall never be found against them forever. They wear the Savior's righteousness, even as they have been washed in His blood; and what wrath can lie on the man who is not only guiltless through the blood of Christ but also meritorious through imputed righteousness! Oh, arm of Justice, you are forbidden to smite the blood-washed saints! Oh, you flames of hell, how could even so much as the breath of your heat pass upon the man who is safely covered in the Savior's wounds! How is it possible for you, O deaths, destructions, horrors, glooms, plagues, and terrors, so much as to flit like a cloud over the serene sky of the spirit that has found peace with God through the blood of Christ! No, brethren:

> Bold shall I stand in that great day;
> For who aught to my charge shall lay?
> While, through thy blood, absolved I am
> From sin's tremendous curse and shame.

There shall be a second death, but it shall have no power over us. Do you understand the beauty of the picture? As if we might walk through the flames of hell and they should have *no power* to devour us any more than when the holy children paced with ease over the hot coals of Nebuchadnezzar's seven times heated furnace. Death may bend his bow and fit the arrow to the string, but we laugh at you, O death! and you, O hell, we will despise! For over both of you enemies of man, we shall be more than conquerors through Him who has loved us. We shall stand invulnerable and invincible, defying and laughing to scorn our every foe. And all this because we are washed from sin and covered with a spotless righteousness.

But there is another reason why the second death can have no power on the believer, because when the prince of this world comes against us then, we shall be able to say what our Master did: "[He] hath nothing in me" (John 14:30). When we shall rise again, we shall be freed from all corruption: no evil tendencies shall remain in us. "I will cleanse their blood that I have not cleansed: for the LORD dwelleth in Zion" (Joel 3:21). "Not having spot, or wrinkle, or any such thing" (Eph. 5:27), without even the shadow of a spot that the eye of omniscience could discover, we shall be as pure as Adam before his fall, as holy as the Immaculate manhood when it first came from the divine hand. We shall be better than Adam, for Adam might sin, but we shall be so established in goodness, in truth, and in righteousness that we shall not even be tempted again, much less shall we have any fear of falling. We shall stand spotless and faultless at the last great day. Brethren, lift up your heads. Contending with sin, cast down with doubts, lift up your heads and wipe the tears from your eyes. There are days coming, the like of which angels have not seen, but you shall see them. There are times coming when your spirits shall no more fear the chain, nor shall you even remember the pain and tears of earth.

There is yet a third privilege in the text. I believe this to be also one of the glories that shall be revealed: *"They shall reign with him a thousand years."* This is another point upon which there has been a long and very vigorous contention. It was believed in the early Church that the seventh thousand years of the world's history would be a Sabbath, that as there were six days of toil in the week, and the seventh was a day of rest, so the world would have six thousand years of toil and sorrow, and the seventh thousand would be a thousand years of rest. I do not know that there is any Scripture that supports this view, but I am also not aware of any verse against it. I believe the Lord Himself shall come, "But of that day and that hour knoweth no man, no, not the angels which are in heaven, neither the Son, but the Father" (Mark 13:32). And I think it is frivolous to attempt to fix even the year or even the century when Christ shall come. Our business is to expect Him always, to be always looking for His appearing, watching for His coming, so that whether He comes at morning, noon, or midnight, we may be ready to go with the wise virgins into the marriage feast and to rejoice with our Beloved. If there have been any dates given, I am not able at present to verify them.

Yet I think we may say there is in the text a distinct promise that the saints are to reign with Christ a thousand years, and I believe they are to reign with Him *upon this earth*. There are some passages that I think obtain a singular fullness of meaning if this is true. Turn to Psalm 37:10–11. It is that psalm where David has been fretting himself because of the evildoers and their prosperity upon the earth. He says, "For yet a little while, and the wicked shall not be: yea, thou shalt diligently consider his place, and it shall not be. But the meek shall inherit the earth; and shall delight themselves in the abundance of peace." You can interpret that to mean that the meek person shall enjoy much more of this world's goods than the sinner and that he shall have abundance of peace. But I think you have given it an inadequate meaning. If it is true that these meek ones shall yet possess this very earth and that here in the abundance of peace through the Messiah's reign they shall rejoice in it, I think you have found a fuller meaning, and one that has a Godlike meaning. So it is that God's promises always have a wider meaning than we can imagine. In this case, if it means only that the meek are to have what they gain and enjoy in this lifetime, which is very little indeed, the promise has a slender meaning. But if it means that they shall have glory even here, you have given to it one of the widest meanings you can imagine, a meaning like the meanings usually given to the promises of God—wide, large, extensive, and worthy of Himself.

We need to realize that the meek do not inherit the earth to any great degree at present, and we look confidently for this in another age. Let me quote the language of Christ lest you should think this passage peculiar to the Old Testament dispensation: "Blessed are the meek: for they shall inherit the earth" (Matt. 5:5). How? Where? When? Not now certainly, not in Christ's days, not in apostolic times by any means. What did the meek inherit? Prisons, flames, racks, beasts, dungeons. Their inheritance, indeed, was nothing. They were destitute, afflicted, tormented; they wandered about in sheepskins and goatskins; and if the meek are ever to inherit the earth, certainly it must be in some age to come, for they have never inherited it yet.

Turn again to a passage in Revelation 5:9–10: "And they sung a new song, saying, Thou art worthy to take the book, and to open the seals thereof: for thou wast slain, and hast redeemed us to God by thy blood out of every kindred, and tongue, and people, and nation; and hast made us unto our God kings and priests: and we shall reign *on the earth*." If these words mean anything at all, if the Holy Spirit meant to set forth any meaning, surely it must have been that the day was coming when the people of Christ shall reign upon the earth. Besides, remember our Savior's words in Matthew 19:28–29, where in answer to a question that had been put by Peter as to what His saints should have as the result of their losses for His sake, He said to them, "Verily I say unto you, That ye which have followed me, in the regeneration when the Son of man shall sit in the throne of his glory, ye also shall sit upon twelve thrones, judging the twelve tribes of Israel. And every one that hath forsaken houses, or brethren, or sisters, or father, or mother, or wife, or children, or lands, for my name's sake, shall receive an hundredfold, and shall inherit everlasting life." It seems clear that Christ is to come in the regeneration, when in a newborn world there shall be joys fitted for the newborn spirits, and then there shall be splendors and glories for the apostles first and for all those who by any means have suffered any losses for Christ Jesus. You find such passages as these in the Word of God. "The LORD of hosts shall reign in mount Zion, and in Jerusalem, and before his ancients gloriously" (Isa. 24:23). You find another like this in Zechariah 14:5: "And the LORD my God shall come, and all the saints with thee." Indeed, I could quote many passages in which it seems to me that nothing but the triumph on the very spot where the saints have fought the battle, nothing but the glory in the very place where they have had the tug of war, will meet the meaning of God's Word. I do look forward to this with joy, that though I may sleep in Christ before my Master comes, yet I shall rise at the day of His appearing and shall be recompensed at the resurrection of the just if I have truly and faithfully served Him, and that recompense shall be to be made like unto Jesus and to partake of His glories before the eyes of men and to reign with Him during the thousand years.

But let me gather up what I have said and make one more observation. This doctrine is not an impractical one. For throughout the New Testament, whenever the biblical writers want to stir up believers to patience, to labor, to hope, to endurance, to holiness, they generally say something about the advent of Christ. "Be ye also patient; stablish your hearts: for the coming of the Lord draweth nigh" (James 5:8). "Let your moderation be known unto all men. The Lord is at hand" (Phil. 4:5). "Judge nothing before the time, until the Lord come" (1 Cor. 4:5). "And when the chief Shepherd shall appear, ye shall receive a crown of glory that fadeth not away" (1 Pet. 5:4). I think we shall do wrong if we make too much of this concept, but we shall do equally wrong if we make too little of it. Let us give it a fair place in our thoughts, and especially let those of us who fear God and believe in Jesus take this to be a window through which we can look; when the house is dark and our home is full of misery, let us look to the time when we shall rise among the first, following Christ the firstfruits, when we shall reign with Christ, sharing in His glories, and when we shall know that the second death has no power over us.

Three Things in Simplicity

If for you the idea of the resurrection of the righteous has no music, or if there is no flash of joy in your spirit when you hear that the dead shall rise again, I pray you will lend me your ear while I assure you in God's name that you shall rise. Not only shall your soul live, but your body itself shall live. Those eyes that have been full of lust shall see sights of horror; those ears that have listened to the temptations of the evil one shall hear the thunders of the day of judgment; those very feet that carried you toward sin shall attempt, but utterly fail, to sustain you when Christ shall sit in judgment. He is able to cast both body and soul into hell. While the heathen often believed in the immortality of the soul, it is the doctrine of the resurrection of the body that is peculiar to Christianity. God's book tells me that all the dead, both small and great, shall rise. When the archangel's trump shall sound, the whole of the old inhabitants of the world before the flood shall arise. The buried palaces, the sunken homes, shall all give up the multitude who once married and were given in marriage until Noah entered into the ark. Every churchyard, too, where men have been quietly buried with Christian rites but yet were non-Christian still, shall yield up its dead. The battlefield shall yield a mighty harvest, a harvest that was sown in blood and shall be reaped in tempest. Every place where man has lived and man has died shall see the dying brought to life once again. But the main thing with you is that *you* will be there. Oh, you may well pamper your body now, but when this short time on earth is over, you shall drink the dregs of the cup of God's wrath. Go your way, eat, drink and be merry, but for all these the Lord shall bring you into judgment. When you enter into sin, think of the resurrection.

But after the resurrection, according to the text, comes *the judgment*. You have cursed God, but the foul word died away. No, it did not; it imprinted itself upon the great book of God's remembrance. You may have entered the chamber of pleasure or the hall of infidelity, you may have walked through the stews of crime and through the stench and filth of the sexually impure. You have wandered into sin and plunged into it, thinking that it would all die with the day, that as the night covers up the sights of the day, so the night of death should cover up the deeds of your day of life. Not so. The books shall be opened. I think I see you closing your eyes because you dare not look upon the Judge when He opens that page where your history stands. I hear the boldest of sinners crying to the sublime and dread granite rocks, "Fall on me." He would rather be crushed than stand there before the avenging eye; but the mountains will not loosen, their flinty bowels feel no pangs of sympathy, they will not move. You stand while the dread voice reads on, and on, and on, your every act and word and thought. I see you as the shameful list is read, and men and angels hear. I see your horror as a nameless deed is told, in terms explicit, that none can misunderstand. I hear your thoughts brought out—that lust, that murder that was in the thought, but never grew into the deed. And you are all this time astonished like Belshazzar, when he saw the writing on the wall and he was terribly afraid. So shall it be with you.

But then comes the end, the last of all. After death, the judgment; after judgment, *the damnation*. If it is to be a dreadful thing to live again, if it is a more dreadful thing still to spend the first day of that life in the grand court of God, how much more awful shall it be when the sentence is pronounced and the terror of punishment shall begin! If you do not fear God and have no faith in Jesus, I cannot picture to you damnation. Across it let me draw a curtain. But though we must not picture it, I pray you realize it. This much we know, that hell is a place of absence from God—a place for the development of sin, where every passion is unbridled, every lust unrestrained—a place where God punishes those who sin, a place where the gospel is denied, where mercy droops her wings and dies—a place, the like of which imagination has not pictured. May God grant it may be a place that you shall never see and whose dread you shall never feel. Let me bid you to fly away from it now while you are still on praying ground. Think of your end, and never let it be said about you as was the case with Jerusalem: "She remembereth not her last end; therefore she came down wonderfully" (Lam. 1:9). Think! Think! This warning may be the last you shall ever hear!

I lift up before you now Christ the crucified one: "Whosoever believeth in him should not perish, but have eternal life" (John 3:15). As Moses lifted up the serpent in the wilderness, so at this very moment the Son of Man is lifted up. See His wounds. Look to His thorn-crowned head. See the nails of His hands and of His feet. Do you perceive Him? Hark! while He cries, "Why hast thou forsaken me?" (Matt. 27:46). Listen again, while He says, "It is finished!" (John 19:30). Salvation is finished! Believe on Christ, and you shall be saved. Trust Him, and all the horrors of the future shall have no power over you; but the splendors of this prophecy shall be fulfilled, be they what they may.

*R*emember, too, that it was always considered to be the duty of the goel not merely to redeem by price but, where that failed, to redeem by power. Hence, when Lot was carried away captive by the four kings, Abraham summoned his own hired servants and the servants of all his friends and went out against the kings of the East and brought back Lot and the captives of Sodom (Gen. 14). Now, our Lord Jesus Christ, who once has played the Kinsman's part by paying the price for us, lives, and He will redeem us by power. O Death, you tremble at His name! You know the might of our Kinsman! Against His arm you cannot stand! You did once meet Him foot to foot in stern battle, and O Death, you did indeed tread upon His heel. He voluntarily submitted to this, or else, O Death, you had no power against Him. But He slew you, Death, He slew you! He rifled all your caskets, took from you the key of your castle, burst open the door of your dungeon. And now, you know, Death, you have no power to hold my body; you may set your slaves to devour it, but you shall give it up, and all their spoil must be restored. Insatiable Death, from your greedy jaws yet shall return the multitudes whom you have devoured. You shall be compelled by the Savior to restore your captives to the light of day. I think I see Jesus coming with His Father's servants. The chariots of the Lord are twenty thousand, even thousands of angels. Blow the trumpet! Blow the trumpet! Emmanuel rides to battle! The Most Mighty in majesty girds on His sword. He comes! By power He comes to snatch His people's lands from those who have invaded their portion. How glorious the victory! No battle shall there be. He comes, He sees, He conquers. The sound of the trumpet shall be enough. Death shall fly away in fright, and instantly from beds of dust and silent clay to realms of everlasting day the righteous shall arise.

Chapter Four

I Know That My Redeemer Liveth

For I know that my redeemer liveth, and that he shall stand at the latter day upon the earth: and though after my skin worms destroy this body, yet in my flesh shall I see God: whom I shall see for myself, and mine eyes shall behold, and not another; though my reins be consumed within me—Job 19:25–27.

JOB'S DECLARATION DESERVES our profound attention. Its preface would hardly have been written had not the matter been of the utmost importance in the judgment of the patriarch who uttered it. Listen to Job's remarkable desire: "Oh that my words were now written! oh that they were printed in a book! That they were graven with an iron pen and lead in the rock for ever!" (Job 19:23–24). Perhaps, hardly aware of the full meaning of the words he was uttering yet his holy soul was impressed with a sense of some weighty revelation concealed within his words, he therefore desired that it might be recorded in a book. He has had his desire, and the Book of books showcases the words of Job. He wished to have them graven on a rock, cut deep into it with an iron pen, and then the lines inlaid with lead; or he would have them engraven, according to the custom of the ancients, upon a sheet of metal so that time might not be able to destroy the inscription. He has not had his desire in that respect except that upon many tombstones those words of Job stand recorded, "I know that my Redeemer liveth." Whether such a sentence adorned the portals of

Job's last sleeping place we know not, but certainly no words could have been more fitly chosen. Should not the man of patience, the mirror of endurance, the pattern of trust, bear as his memorial this golden line, which is as full of all the patience of hope, and hope of patience, as mortal language can be? Who among us could select a more glorious motto for his last insignia?

Let Us Descend in the Sepulcher

The body has just been divorced from the soul. Friends who loved most tenderly have said, "Bury my dead out of my sight." The body is borne upon the bier and consigned to the silent earth; it is surrounded by the earthworks of death. Death has a host of troops. If the locusts and the caterpillars are God's army, the worms are the army of Death. These hungry warriors begin to attack the city of man. They commence with the outer walls, then they storm the strongholds and overturn the walls. The skin, the city wall of manhood, is utterly broken down, and the towers of its glory covered with confusion. How speedily the cruel invaders deface all beauty. Alas, you windows of agates and gates of carbuncle, where are you now? How shall I mourn for you, O captive city, for the mighty have utterly spoiled you! Where is beauty now? The most lovely cannot be known from the most deformed. The vessel so daintily wrought upon the potter's wheel is cast away upon the dunghill with the vilest potsherds. Cruel have you been, you warriors of death, for though you wield no axes and bear no hammers, yet have you broken down the carved work; and though you speak not with tongues, yet have you said in your hearts, "We have swallowed her up; certainly this is the day that we have looked for." No matter how artistic the work might be—and certainly we are fearfully and wonderfully made, and the anatomist stands still and marvels to see the skill that the eternal God has manifested in the formation of the body—but these ruthless worms pull everything to pieces till, like a city sacked and spoiled that has been given up for days to pillage and to flame, everything lies in a heap of ruin—ashes to ashes, dust to dust. It is gone, it is all gone! The skin, the body, the organs, all, all has departed. There is nothing left. In a few years you shall turn up the sod and say, "Here slept so-and-so, and where is he now?" and you may search and hunt and dig, but you shall find no relic. Mother Earth has devoured her own offspring.

Why should we wish to have it otherwise? Why should we desire to preserve the body when the soul has gone? What vain attempts men have made with coffins of lead and wrappings of myrrh and frankincense. The embalming of the Egyptians, those master robbers of the worm, what has it done? It has served to keep some poor shriveled lumps of mortality above ground to be sold for curiosities, to be dragged away to foreign museums, and stared upon by thoughtless eyes. No, let the dust go, the sooner it dissolves the better. It is ordained that somehow or other it must be all separated—"dust to dust, ashes to ashes." It is part of the decree that it should all perish.

Do not seek to avoid what God has purposed; do not look upon it as a gloomy thing. Regard it as a necessity; nay more, view it as the platform of a miracle, the lofty stage of resurrection, since Jesus shall surely raise again from the dead the particles of this body, however divided from one another. We have heard of miracles, but what a miracle is the resurrection! All the miracles of Scripture, yes even those wrought by Christ, are small compared with this.

I think very much of the essence of Job's faith lay in this, that he had a clear view that the worms would after his skin destroy his body, and yet that in his flesh he should see God. You know we might regard it as a small miracle if we could preserve the bodies of the departed. If, by some process, we could preserve the particles, for the Lord to make those dry bones live and to quicken that skin and flesh were a miracle certainly but not palpably and plainly so great a marvel as when the worms have destroyed the body. When the fabric has been absolutely broken up, the tenement all pulled down, ground to pieces, and flung in handfuls to the wind so that no relic of it is left, and yet when Christ stands in the latter days upon the earth, all the structure shall be brought together, bone to bone—then shall the might of omnipotence be seen. This is the doctrine of the resurrection, and happy is he who finds no difficulty here, who looks at it as being an impossibility with man but a possibility with God, and who lays hold upon the omnipotence of the Most High and says, "Thou sayest it, and it shall be done!"

Let Us Look Up to Our Hope

"I know," said Job, "that my Redeemer liveth." The word *Redeemer* is in the original *goel*—meaning *kinsman*. The duty of the kinsman, or *goel*, was very specific. Suppose an Israelite had alienated his estate, as in the case of Naomi and Ruth, and it had passed away through poverty. It was then the goel's business, the redeemer's business, to pay the price as the next of kin and to buy back the heritage. Boaz stood in that relation to Ruth. Now, the body may be looked upon as the heritage of the soul—the soul's small farm, that little plot of earth in which the soul has been accustomed to walk and delight, as a man walks in his garden or dwells in his house. Then, Death takes away the property from us and we lose our estate. Death also sends his troops to ruin our body. But we turn round to Death and say, "I know that my Goel liveth, and He will redeem this heritage. I have lost it; you took it from me lawfully, O Death, because my sin has forfeited my right. I have lost my heritage through my own offense and through that of my first parent Adam, but there lives One who will buy this back."

Job could say this of Christ long before Jesus descended upon earth: "I know that He liveth." And now that Christ has ascended up on high and led captivity captive, surely we may with double emphasis say, "I know that my Goel, my Kinsman lives, and that He has paid the price, that I should have back my estate, so that in my flesh I shall see God." Yes, my hands, you are redeemed with blood, bought not with corruptible things, as with silver and gold, but with the precious blood of Christ. Yes, heaving lungs and palpitating heart, you have been redeemed! He who redeemed the soul to be His altar has also redeemed the body, that it may be a temple for the Holy Ghost. Not even the bones of Joseph can remain in the house of Egyptian bondage. No smell of the fire of death may pass upon the garments that His holy children have worn in the furnace.

Remember, too, that it was always considered to be the duty of the goel not merely to redeem by price but, where that failed, to redeem by power. Hence, when Lot was carried away captive by the four kings, Abraham summoned his own hired servants and the servants of all his friends and went out against the kings of the East and brought back Lot and the captives of Sodom (Gen. 14). Now, our Lord Jesus Christ, who once has played the Kinsman's part by paying the price for us, lives, and He will redeem us by power. O Death, you tremble at His name! You know the might of our Kinsman! Against His arm you cannot stand! You did once meet Him foot to foot in stern battle, and O Death, you did indeed tread upon His heel. He voluntarily submitted to this, or else, O Death, you had no power against Him. But He slew you, Death, He slew you! He rifled all your caskets, took from you the key of your castle, burst open the door of your dungeon. And now, you know, Death, you have no power to hold my body; you may set your slaves to devour it, but you shall give it up, and all their spoil must be restored. Insatiable Death, from your greedy jaws yet shall return the multitudes whom you have devoured. You shall be compelled by the Savior to restore your captives to the light of day. I think I see Jesus coming with His Father's servants. The chariots of the Lord are twenty thousand, even thousands of angels. Blow the trumpet! Blow the trumpet! Emmanuel rides to battle! The Most Mighty in majesty girds on His sword. He comes! By power He comes to snatch His people's lands from those who have invaded their portion. How glorious the victory! No battle shall there be. He comes, He sees, He conquers. The sound of the trumpet shall be enough. Death shall fly away in fright, and instantly from beds of dust and silent clay to realms of everlasting day the righteous shall arise.

To linger here a moment, there was yet, very conspicuously in the Old Testament, we are informed, a third duty of the goel, which was to avenge the death of his friend. If a person had been slain, the goel was the avenger of blood; snatching up his sword, he at once pursued the person who had been guilty of bloodshed. So now, let us picture ourselves as being smitten by Death. His arrow has just pierced us to the heart, but in the act of expiring, our lips are able to boast of vengeance, and in the face of the monster we cry, "I know that my Goel lives." You may fly, O Death, as rapidly as you will, but no city of refuge can hide you from Him. He will overtake you and lay hold upon you, O you skeleton monarch, and He will avenge my blood on you. I would that I had powers of eloquence to work out this magnificent thought. Magnificent preachers such as Chrysostom or Christmas Evans could picture the flight of the King of Terrors, the pursuit by the Redeemer, the overtaking of the foe, and the slaying of the destroyer. Christ shall certainly avenge Himself on Death for all the injury that Death has done to His beloved kinsmen. Comfort yourself then, O Christian; you have ever living, even when you die, One who avenges you, One who has paid the price for you, and One whose strong arms shall yet set you free.

Passing on in our text to notice the next word, it seems that Job found consolation not only in the fact that he had a Goel, a Redeemer, but also in the fact that this Redeemer lives. Job does not say, "I know that my Goel *shall live*," but he says, "He *lives*," having a clear view of the self-existence of the Lord Jesus Christ, the same yesterday, today, and forever. And you and I looking back do not say, "I know that He *did live*," but say, "He *lives* today." This very day you who mourn and sorrow for venerated friends, your prop and pillar in years gone by, you may go to Christ with confidence because He not only lives but also is the source of life, and you therefore believe that He can give eternal life to those whom you have committed to the tomb. He is the Lord and giver of life originally, and He shall be specially declared to be the resurrection and the life when the legions of His redeemed shall be glorified with Him. If I saw no fountain from which life could stream to the dead, I would yet believe the promise when God said that the dead shall live; but when I see the fountain provided and know that it is full to the brim and that it runs over, I can rejoice without trembling. Since there is One who can say, "I am the resurrection, and the life" (John 11:25), it is a blessed thing to see the means already before us in the person of our Lord Jesus Christ.

Still the root of Job's comfort seems to lie in that little word *my*. "I know that *my* Redeemer liveth." Oh, to get hold of Christ! I know that in His offices He is precious. But we must be connected to Him before we can really enjoy Him. What is honey in the wood to me if like the Israelites I dare not eat it. It is honey in my hand, honey on my lip, that enlightens my eyes like those of Jonathan (1 Sam. 14:43). What is gold in the mine to me? It is gold in my purse that will satisfy my necessities, purchasing the bread I need. So, what is a kinsman if he is not a kinsman to me? A redeemer who does not redeem me, an avenger who will never stand up for my blood, of what avail were such? But Job's faith was strong and firm in the conviction that the Redeemer was his. Can you say, "I know that *my* Redeemer liveth"?

There is another word in this consoling sentence that no doubt served to give a zest to the comfort of Job. It was that he could say, "I KNOW—I KNOW that my Redeemer liveth." To say, "I hope so, I trust so," is comfortable, and there are thousands in the fold of Jesus who hardly ever get much further. But to reach the heart of consolation you *must* say, "I KNOW." Ifs, buts, and perhapses are sure murderers of peace and comfort. Doubts are dreary things in times of sorrow. Like wasps they sting the soul! If I have any suspicion that Christ is not mine, there is vinegar mingled with the gall of death. But if I know that Jesus is mine, darkness is not dark; even the night is light about me. "I know that my Redeemer liveth." This is a brightly burning lamp cheering the darkness of the sepulchral vault, but a feeble hope is like a flickering smoking flax, just making darkness visible, but nothing more. I would not like to die with a mere hope mingled with suspicion. I might be safe with this but hardly happy; but oh, to go down into the river of death knowing that all is well, confident that as a guilty, weak, and helpless creature I have fallen into the arms of Jesus, and believing that He is able to keep that which I have committed to Him.

I would have you never look upon the full assurance of faith as a thing impossible to you. Say not, "It is too high; I cannot attain unto it." I have known one or two saints of God who have rarely doubted their interest at all. There are many of us who do not often enjoy any ravishing spiritual ecstasies, but on the other hand we generally maintain the even tenor of our way, simply hanging onto Christ, feeling that His promise is true, that His merits are sufficient, and that we are safe. Assurance is a jewel for worth but not for rarity. It is the common privilege of all the saints if they have but the grace to attain to it, and this grace the Holy Spirit gives freely. Surely if Job, in those dark misty ages when there was only the morning star and not the sun, when they saw but little, when life and immortality had not been brought to light—if Job before the coming and advent of Christ still could say, "*I know,*" you and I should not speak less positively. God forbid that our positiveness should be presumption. Let us try ourselves and see that our marks and evidences are true lest we form an ungrounded hope, for nothing can be more destructive than to say, "Peace, peace, where there is no peace" (Jer. 6:14).

The Anticipation of Future Delight

Let me call to your remembrance the other part of the text. Job not only knew that the Redeemer lived but also anticipated the time when he should *stand in the latter day upon the earth.* No doubt Job referred here to our Savior's first advent, to the time when Jesus Christ, the Goel, the Kinsman, should stand upon the earth to pay in the blood of His veins the ransom price that had, indeed, in bond and stipulation been paid before the foundation of the world in promise.

But I cannot think that Job's vision stayed there. Job was looking forward to the second coming of Christ as being the period of the resurrection. We are persuaded that "the latter day" refers to the advent of glory rather than to that of shame. Our hope is that the Lord shall come to reign in glory where He once died in agony. The bright and hallowed doctrine of the second advent has been greatly revived in our churches in these latter days, and I look for the best results in consequence. There is always a danger lest it be perverted and turned by fanatical minds, by prophetic speculations, into an abuse; but the doctrine in itself is one of the most consoling and, at the same time, one of the most practical, tending to keep the Christian awake, because the Bridegroom comes at such an hour as we think not.

Beloved, we believe that the same Jesus who ascended from Olivet shall so come in like manner as He ascended up into heaven. We believe in His personal advent and reign. We believe and expect that when both wise and foolish virgins shall slumber, in the night when sleep is heavy upon the saints, when men shall be eating and drinking as in the days of Noah, that suddenly as the lightning flashes from heaven, so Christ shall descend with a shout, and the dead in Christ shall rise and reign with Him. We are looking forward to the literal, personal, and actual standing of Christ upon earth as the time when creation's groans shall be silenced forever and the earnest expectation of the creature shall be fulfilled.

Note that Job describes Christ as *standing*. Some interpreters have read the passage, "he shall stand in the latter days *against* the earth"; that as the earth has covered up the slain, as the earth has become the mortuary of the dead, Jesus shall arise to the contest and say, "Earth, I am against you; give up your dead! You clods of the valley cease to be custodians of My people's bodies! Silent deeps, and you caverns of the earth, deliver, once for all, those whom you have imprisoned!" Macphelah shall give up its precious treasure, cemeteries and graveyards shall release their captives, and all the deep places of the earth shall relinquish the bodies of the faithful. Well, whether this interpretation is correct or not, the posture of Christ in standing upon the earth is significant. It shows His triumph. He has triumphed over sin, which once like a serpent in its coils had bound the earth. He has defeated Satan. On the very spot where Satan gained his power, Christ has gained the victory.

Earth, that was a scene of defeated goodness, where mercy once was all but driven, where virtue died, where everything heavenly and pure, like flowers blasted by pestilential winds, hung down their heads, withered and blighted—on this very earth everything that is glorious shall grow and blossom in perfection; and Christ himself, once despised and rejected of men, fairest of all the sons of men, shall come in the midst of a crowd of courtiers, while kings and princes shall do Him homage and all the nations shall call Him blessed. "He shall stand in the latter day upon the earth."

Then, at that auspicious hour, says Job, "In my flesh I shall see God." Oh, blessed anticipation—"I shall see God." He does not say, "I shall see the saints"—doubtless we shall see them all in heaven—but says, "I shall see *God*." Note he does not say, "I shall see the pearly gates, I shall see the walls of jasper, I shall see the crowns of gold and the harps of harmony," but says, "I shall see God," as if that were the sum and substance of heaven. "In my flesh shall I see *God*." The pure in heart shall see God. It was their delight to see Him in the ordinances by faith. They delighted to behold Him in communion and in prayer. There in heaven they shall have a vision of another sort. We shall see God in heaven and be made completely like Him; the divine character shall be stamped upon us; and being made like Him, we shall be perfectly satisfied and content. Likeness to God, what can we wish for more? And a sight of God, what can we desire better? We shall see God, and so there shall be perfect contentment to the soul and a satisfaction of all the faculties.

Some read the passage, "Yet, I shall see God in my flesh," and think that this is an allusion to Christ, our Lord Jesus Christ, as "the word made flesh." Well, whether it be so or not, it is certain that we shall see Christ, and He, as the divine Redeemer, shall be the subject of our eternal vision. Nor shall we ever want any joy beyond simply that of seeing Him. Think not that this will be a narrow sphere for your mind to dwell in. It is but one source of delight, "I shall see God," but that source is infinite. His wisdom, His love, His power, all His attributes shall be subjects for your eternal contemplation, and as He is infinite under each aspect, there is no fear of exhaustion. His works, His purposes, His gifts, His love to you, and His glory in all His purposes and in all His deeds of love—why, these shall make a theme that never can be exhausted. You may with divine delight anticipate the time when in your flesh you shall see God.

But I must have you observe how Job has expressly made us note that it is in the same body. "Yet, *in my flesh* shall I see God"; and then he says again, "whom I shall see for myself, and mine eye shall behold and not another." Yes, it is true that I, the very man writing these words, though I must go down to die, yet I shall as the same man most certainly arise and shall behold my God. Not part of myself, though the soul alone shall have some view of God, but the whole of myself—my flesh, my soul, my body, my spirit— shall gaze on God. We shall not enter heaven as a dismasted vessel is tugged into harbor: we shall not get to glory with some on boards and some on broken pieces of the ship, but the whole ship shall be floated safely into the haven, body and soul both being safe. Christ shall be able to say, *"All* that the Father giveth me shall come to me" (John 6:37), not only all the persons but also all of the persons—each person in his perfection. There shall not be found in heaven one imperfect saint. There shall not be a saint without an eye, much less a saint without a body. No member of the body shall have perished, nor shall the body have lost any of its natural beauty. All the saints shall be all there, and all of all, the same persons precisely, only that they shall have risen from a state of grace to a state of glory.

Please notice how the patriarch puts it as being a real personal enjoyment. "Whom mine eyes shall behold, and not another." They shall not bring me a report as they did the Queen of Sheba, but I shall see Solomon the king for myself. I shall be able to say, as they did who spoke to the woman of Samaria, "Now we believe, not because of thy saying: for we have heard him ourselves, and know that this is indeed the Christ, the Saviour of the world" (John 4:42). There shall be personal fellowship with God, not through the Book, which is but as a glass, nor through the ordinances, but directly, in the person of our Lord Jesus Christ, we shall be able to commune with the Father as a man talks with his friend. "Not another." If my heaven must be enjoyed by proxy, if draughts of bliss must be drunk for me, where were the hope? Oh, no; for myself, and not through another, shall I see God. Nothing but personal religion will do, because resurrection and glory are personal things. "Not another." If you could have sponsors to repent for you, then, depend upon it, you would have sponsors to be glorified for you. But as there is not another to see God for you, so you must yourself see and yourself find an interest in the Lord Jesus Christ.

In closing, let me observe how foolish have you and I been when we have looked forward to death with shudders, with doubts, with loathings. After all, what is it? Worms! Do you tremble at those base crawling things? Scattered particles! Shall we be alarmed at these? To meet the worms we have the angels, and to gather the scattered particles we have the voice of God. I am sure the gloom of death is altogether gone now that the lamp of resurrection burns. Disrobing is nothing now that better garments await us. We may long for evening to undress, that we may rise with God. I am sure my venerable friends now present, in coming so near as they do now to the time of the departure, must have some visions of the glory on the other side of the stream.

John Bunyan was not wrong when he put the land Beulah at the close of the pilgrimage. Is not my text a telescope that will enable you to see across the Jordan; may it not be as hands of angels to bring you bundles of myrrh and frankincense? You can say, "I know that my Redeemer liveth." You cannot want more; you were not satisfied with less in your youth, you will not be content with less now. Those of us who are young are comforted by the thought that we may soon depart. I say comforted, not alarmed by it; and we almost envy those whose race is nearly run, because we fear—and yet we must not speak this way, for the Lord's will be done—I was about to say, we fear that our battle may last long and that perhaps our feet may slip; but He who keeps Israel does not slumber or sleep. So since we know that our Redeemer lives, this shall be our comfort in life, that though we fall we shall not be utterly cast down, and since our Redeemer lives, this shall be our comfort in death, that though worms destroy this body, yet in our flesh we shall see God.

Oh, sirs, consider this word—hereafter! I would gladly whisper it in the ear of the sinner, fascinated by his own pleasures. Come near and let me do so—hereafter! I would make it the alarm of the sleeping transgressor who is dreaming of peace and safety while he is slumbering himself into hell. Hereafter! Hereafter! Oh, yes, you may suck the sweet and eat the fat and drink as you will, but hereafter! hereafter! What will you do hereafter when that which is sweet in the mouth shall be as gall in the belly and when the pleasures of today shall be a mixture of misery for eternity? Hereafter! Oh, hereafter! Now, O Spirit divine, be pleased to open careless ears, that they may listen to this prophetic sound.

Chapter Five

Nevertheless, Hereafter

Jesus saith unto him, Thou hast said: nevertheless I say unto you, Hereafter shall ye see the Son of man sitting on the right hand of power, and coming in the clouds of heaven—Matthew 26:64.

OUR LORD BEFORE HIS ENEMIES was silent in His own defense, but He faithfully warned and boldly held to the truth. His was the silence of patience, not of indifference; of courage, not of cowardice. It is written that "before Pontius Pilate [he] witnessed a good confession" (1 Tim. 6:13), and that statement may also be well applied to His utterances before Caiaphas, for there He was not silent when it came to the confession of necessary truth.

If you will read Matthew 26, you will notice that the high priest adjured Him, saying, "Tell us whether thou be the Christ, the Son of God," to which He replied at once, "Thou hast said [it]" (vv. 63–64). Jesus did not disown His Messiahship. He claimed to be the Promised One, the Messenger from heaven, Christ the Anointed of the Most High. Neither did He for a moment renounce His personal deity: He acknowledged and confessed that He was the Son of God. How could He be silent when such a vital point as to His person was in question? He did not hold them in suspense but openly declared His Godhead by saying, "I am." He then proceeded to reveal the solemn fact that He would soon sit at the right hand of God, even the Father.

In the words of our next text, He declared that those who were condemning Him would see Him glorified and in due time would stand at His judgment bar when He would come upon the clouds of heaven to judge the quick and dead according to our gospel. Note the great truths of our holy faith clearly set forth by our Lord Jesus: He claimed to be the Christ of God and the Son of God, and His brief statement by implication speaks of His death, burial, and resurrection to be enthroned at the right hand of God in the power of the Father and soon to come in His glorious second advent to judge the world in righteousness. Our Lord's confession was very comprehensive, and happy is he who heartily embraces it.

I intend to dwell upon three significant words around which is gathered a world of encouraging and solemn thought. The first is *nevertheless*, and the second is *hereafter*; what the third is you shall know hereafter, but not just now.

Nevertheless

"Thou hast said: nevertheless I say unto you," said Christ, "Hereafter shall ye see the Son of man sitting on the right hand of power, and coming in the clouds of heaven." This, then, is the string from which we must draw forth music. *Nevertheless* signifies that truth is nevertheless sure because of opposition. "Nevertheless," not one atom the less is the truth certain to prevail for all that you say or do against it. Jesus will surely sit at the right hand of power and come in due season upon the clouds of heaven despite the opposition of men and devils.

Observe, first, that *the Savior's condition when He made use of that "nevertheless" was no proof that He could not rise in power.* There Jesus stood, a poor, defenseless man, newly led from the night watch in the garden of Gethsemane and its bloody sweat. *He was a spectacle of meek and lowly suffering,* led by His captors like a lamb to the slaughter, with none to speak a word on His behalf. He was surrounded by those who hated Him, and He was forsaken by His friends. Scribes, Pharisees, and priests were all thirsting for His heart's blood.

A lamb in the midst of wolves is but a faint picture of Christ standing there before the Sanhedrin in patient silence. And yet, though His present condition seemed to contradict it, He who was the faithful and true witness spoke truly when He testified, "Nevertheless, hereafter shall ye see the Son of man coming in the clouds of heaven. Despite My present shame and suffering, so it shall be."

He gives Himself that humble title of Son of Man, as best indicating Himself in His condition at that time. "Hereafter shall ye see the Son of man sitting on the right hand of power, and coming in the clouds of heaven." The humiliation of Christ did not in the least endanger His later glory. His sufferings, His shame, His death did not render it any the less certain that He would climb to His throne. Nor did the jests of His opposers keep Him for one instant from His place of honor. I wish you to remember this, for there is a great principle in it.

There are many cowardly people who cannot take sides with a persecuted truth or accept anything but the most popular and fashionable form of religion. They dare not side with truth when men spit in its face and buffet it and pour contempt upon it; but it will be victorious nonetheless, although cowards desert it and false-hearted men oppose it. If it stand alone at the judgment seat of the world, a culprit to be condemned, if it receive nothing but a universal hiss of human abhorrence—yet, if it is the truth, it may be condemned, but it will be justified; it may be buried, but it will rise; it may be rejected, but it will be glorified, even as it has happened to the Christ of God.

Who would be ashamed of truth at any time when he knows the preciousness of it? Who will tremble because of present opposition when he foresees what will yet come of it? What a sublime spectacle—the Man of sorrows standing before His cruel judges in all manner of weakness and poverty and contempt, at the same time heir of all things and appointed, nevertheless, to sit at the right hand of power and to come in the clouds of heaven.

Nor may we think only of His condition as a despised and rejected man, for He was, on His trial, charged with grievous wrong and about to be *condemned by the ecclesiastical authorities*. The scribes skilled in the law declared that He blasphemed, and the priests, familiar with the ordinances of God, exclaimed, "Away with Him. He must not be allowed to live." The high priest himself gave judgment that it was expedient for Him to be put to death. It is a very serious thing, is it not, when all the ecclesiastical authorities are against you—when they are unanimous in your condemnation?

Yes, truly, and it may cause great searching of heart, for no peace-able man desires to be opposed to constituted authority but would sooner have the good word of those who sit in Moses' seat. But this was not the last time in which the established religious authorities were wrong, grievously wrong. They were condemning the inno-cent and blaspheming the Lord from heaven. Nor, I say, was this the last time in which the world's religious leaders have been upon the side of cruel wrong: yet this did not un-Christ our Savior or rob Him of His deity or His throne.

Human history brings before us an abundance of instances in which, though scribes, priests, bishops, pontiffs, and popes con-demned the truth, it was just as sure and became as triumphant as it had a right to do. There stands the one lone Man, and there are all the great ones around Him—men of authority and reputation, sanctity and pomp—and they unanimously deny that He can ever sit at the right hand of God. "But, nevertheless," Jesus said, "here-after shall ye see the Son of man on the right hand of power." He spoke the truth, for His declaration has been most gloriously ful-filled. Even thus over the neck of clergy, priests, pontiffs, popes, His triumphant chariot of salvation shall still roll, and the truth— the simple truth of His glorious gospel—shall, despite them all, win the day and reign over the sons of men.

Nor is this all. Our Lord at that time was *surrounded by those who were in possession of earthly power*. The priests had the ear of Pilate, and Pilate had the Roman legions at his back. Who could resist such a combination of force? Craft and authority form a dreadful league. One disciple drew a sword, but just at the time when our Lord stood before the Sanhedrin, that one chivalrous warrior had denied Him, so that all the physical force was on the other side. As a man, Jesus was helpless when He stood bound before the council. I am not speaking now of that almighty power that faith knows to have dwelt in Him, but as to human power, He was weakness at its weakest. His cause seemed at the lowest ebb. He had none to stand up in His defense—none to speak a word on His behalf, for, "Who shall declare his generation?" (Acts 8:33).

And yet, for all that, and even because of it, He did rise to sit at the right hand of power, and He shall come in the clouds of heaven. So if it ever comes to pass that you should be the lone advocate of a forgotten truth—if your Master should ever put you in all your weakness in the midst of the mighty and the strong, do not fear or tremble, for the possession of power is but a trifle compared with the possession of truth, and he who has the right may safely defy the might of the world. He shall win and conquer, let the princes and powers that be take to themselves what force and craft they choose. Jesus, nevertheless, wins, though the power is all against Him, and so shall the truth that He represents, for it wears about it a hidden power that baffles all opponents.

Nor was it merely all the power; there was *a great deal of furious rage against Him.* That Caiaphas, how he spoke to Him! "I adjure thee," he said, "by the living God." And after he has spoken, Caiaphas rends his garments in indignation, his anger burns like fire; but the Christ is very quiet, the Lamb of God is still, and looking His adversary in the face, He says, "Nevertheless, hereafter thou shalt see the Son of man sitting at the right hand of power, and coming in the clouds of heaven." Jesus was strong and therefore calm, confident and therefore peaceful, fully assured and therefore patient. He could wait, for He believed, and His prophecy was true, notwithstanding the high priest's rage. So if we meet with any man at any time who gnashes his teeth upon us, who foams in passion, who dips his pen in the bitterest gall to write down our holy faith, who is untiring in his violent efforts against the Christ of God—what does it matter? "Nevertheless, ye shall see the Son of man sitting at the right hand of power." "Yet have I set my king upon my holy hill of Zion," said Jehovah (Ps. 2:6), and He declared the decree though the heathen raged and the people imagined a vain thing. Well may a person smile at rage when he is sure of victory.

But it was not merely one person that raged. The people of Jerusalem and the multitudes who had come up to the Passover were bribed and egged on by the priests and the Pharisees. They were all hot after our Savior's death, clamoring, "Crucify him, Crucify him"; and yet there He stood, and as He heard their tumult and anticipated its growing demand for His blood, He lost not His confidence, but He calmly said, "Nevertheless, hereafter, shall ye see the Son of man sitting on the right hand of power."

Beloved, you know that after He had said this, our Lord was taken before Herod and Pilate and at last was put to death: and He knew all this, foreseeing it most clearly, and yet it did not make Him hesitate. He knew that He would be crucified and that His enemies would boast that there was an end of Him and of His kingdom. He knew that His disciples would hide themselves in holes and corners and that nobody would dare to say a word concerning the man of Nazareth. He knew that the name of the Nazarene would be bandied about amid general disgrace, and Jerusalem would say, "That cause has been thoroughly crushed out." But He, foreseeing all that and more, declared, "Nevertheless, hereafter shall ye see the Son of man sitting on the right hand of power."

I cannot help harping upon the text—I hope I shall not weary you with it, for to me it is music. I do not like running over the word *nevertheless* too quickly. I like to draw it out and repeat it as "never-the-less." No, not one jot the less will His victory come. Not in the least degree was His royal power endangered or His sure triumph imperiled. Not even by His death and the consequent scattering of His disciples was the least hazard occasioned; but, indeed, all these things worked together for the accomplishment of the divine purpose concerning Him, and the lower He stooped, the more sure He was to rise ultimately to His glory.

Before long He will come. We cannot tell when: He may come tonight or not for many a weary year: but He will surely come in person, for did not the angels say to the men of Galilee, as they stood gazing into heaven, "This same Jesus, which is taken up from you into heaven, shall so come in like manner as ye have seen him go into heaven" (Acts 1:11)? He shall come with blast of trumpet and with thousands of angelic beings, all doing Him honor. He shall come with flaming fire to visit the trembling earth. He shall come with all His Father's glories on, and kings and princes shall stand before Him, and He shall reign among His ancients gloriously. The tumults of the people and the plottings of their ruler shall be remembered in that day, but it shall be to their own eternal shame. Jesus' throne shall be none the less resplendent.

I beg you to learn the spiritual lesson that comes out of this— never be afraid to stand by a losing cause. Never hesitate to stand alone when the truth is to be confessed. Never be overawed by ecclesiastical power or daunted by rage or swayed by multitudes. Truth may be unpopular, but it is eternal, and that doctrine that is scouted and cast out as evil today shall bring immortal honor to the man who dares to stand by its side and share its humiliation.

Oh, for the love of the Christ who thus threw a "*nevertheless*" at the feet of His foes, follow Him wherever He goes. Through flood or flame, in loneliness, in shame, in obloquy, in reproach, follow Him! If it leads outside the camp, follow Him! If every step shall cost you abuse and scorn, follow still; yea, to prison and to death still follow Him, for as surely as He sits at the right hand of power so shall those who love Him and have been faithful to His truth sit down upon His throne with Him. His overcoming and enthronement are the pledges of the victory both of the truth and of those who courageously champion it.

Thus have we sounded our first great bell—"Nevertheless." Let its music ring through the place and charm each opened ear.

Hereafter

"Nevertheless, hereafter." I like the sound of those two bells together: let us ring them again. "Nevertheless, *hereafter*." The hereafter seems in brief to say to me that *the main glory of Christ lies in the future*. Not today, perhaps, nor tomorrow will the issue be seen! Have patience! Wait awhile: "Their strength is to sit still" (Isa. 30:7). God has great leisure, for He is the Eternal. Let us partake in His restfulness while we sing, *"Nevertheless, hereafter."* Oh, for the Holy Spirit's power at this moment, for it is written, "He will shew you things to come" (John 16:13).

One great reason why the unregenerate sons of men cannot see any glory in the kingdom of Christ is that to them it is such a future thing. Its hopes look into eternity: its great rewards are beyond this present time and state, and the most of mortal eyes cannot see so far. Unregenerate men are like Passion in John Bunyan's parable: they will have all their good things now, and so they have their toys and break them, and they are gone, and then their hereafter is a dreary outlook of regret and woe.

Men of faith know better, and like Patience in the same parable, they choose to have their best things last, for that which comes last, lasts on forever. He whose turn comes last has none to follow him, and his good things shall never be taken away from him. The poor world cannot see beyond its own nose, and so it must have its joys and riches at once. To them speedy victory is the main thing, and the truth is nothing. Is the cause triumphant today? *Off* with your caps, and throw them up, and cry "Hurrah!" no matter that it is the cause of a lie. Do the multitudes incline that way? Then, sir, if you are worldly-wise, run with them. Pull off the palm branches, strew the roads, and shout "Hosanna to the hero of the hour!" though he is a despot or a deceiver.

Not so with those who are taught of God. They take eternity into their estimate, and they are content to go with the despised and rejected of men for the present, because they remember the hereafter. They can swim against the flood, for they know where the course of this world is tending. O blind world, if you were wise, you would revise your line of action and begin to think of the hereafter, too, for, brethren, the hereafter will soon be *here*. What a short time it is since Adam walked in the garden of Eden: compared with the ages of the rocks, compared with the history of the stars, compared with the life of God, it is as the winking of an eye or as a flash of lightning. One has but to grow a little older, and years become shorter and time appears to travel at a much faster rate than before, so that a year rushes by you like a meteor across the midnight heavens.

When we are older still and look down from the serene abodes above, I suppose that centuries and ages will be as moments to us, for to the Lord they are as nothing. Suppose the coming of the Lord should be put off for ten thousand years. When the august spectacle of Christ coming on the clouds of heaven shall really be seen, the delay will be as though but an hour had intervened. The space between now and then, or rather the space between what is "now" at this time and what will be "now" at the last—how short a span it is! Men will look back from the eternal world and say, "How could we have thought so much of the fleeting life we have lived on earth, when it was to be followed by eternity? What fools we were to put so much importance on momentary, transient pleasures, when now the things that are not seen and are eternal have come upon us, and we are unprepared for them!"

Christ will soon come, and at the longest, when He comes, the interval between today and then will seem to be just nothing at all, so that "hereafter" is not as the sound of far-off cannon nor as the boom of distant thunder, but it is the rolling of rushing wheels hastening to overtake us.

"Hereafter!" "Hereafter!" Oh, when that hereafter comes, how overwhelming it will be to Jesus' foes! Now where is Caiaphas? Will he now adjure the Lord to speak? Now, you priests, lift up your haughty heads! Utter a sentence against Him now! There sits your victim upon the clouds of heaven. Say now that He blasphemes and hold up your rent rags and condemn Him again.

But where is Caiaphas? He hides his guilty head: he is utterly confounded and begs the mountains to fall upon him. And, oh, you men of the Sanhedrin, who sat at midnight and glared on your innocent victim with your cold, cruel eyes and afterward gloated over the death of your martyred Prince, where are you now—now that He has come with all His Father's power to judge you? They are asking the hills to open their caverns and conceal them: the rocks deny them shelter. And where, on that day, will you be, you who deny His deity, who profane His Sabbath, who slander His people and denounce His gospel? Where will you be in that tremendous day that as surely comes as comes tomorrow's rising sun?

Oh, sirs, consider this word—*hereafter*! I would gladly whisper it in the ear of the sinner, fascinated by his own pleasures. Come near and let me do so—*hereafter*! I would make it the alarm of the sleeping transgressor who is dreaming of peace and safety while he is slumbering himself into hell. Hereafter! Hereafter! Oh, yes, you may suck the sweet and eat the fat and drink as you will, but hereafter! hereafter! What will you do hereafter when that which is sweet in the mouth shall be as gall in the belly and when the pleasures of today shall be a mixture of misery for eternity? Hereafter! Oh, hereafter! Now, O Spirit divine, be pleased to open careless ears, that they may listen to this prophetic sound.

To the Lord's own people there is no sound more sweet than that of "hereafter." "Hereafter ye shall see the Son of man coming in the clouds of heaven." Welcome, welcome, welcome, welcome, Redeemer, Savior! Welcome in every character in which You come. What acclamations and congratulations will go up from the countless myriads of His redeemed when first the signs of the Son of Man shall be seen in the heavens!

On one of earth's coming mornings, when the children of men shall be "marrying and giving in marriage" (Matt. 24:38), while saints shall be looking for His appearing, they shall first of all perceive that He is actually coming. Long desired, and come at last. Then the trumpet shall be heard, growing exceeding loud and long, ringing out a sweeter note to the true Israel than ever trumpet heard on the morning of Jubilee.

What delight! What lifting up of joyous eyes! What floods of bliss! Oppression is over, the idols are broken, the reign of sin is ended, darkness shall no more cover the nations. He comes, He comes: glory be to His name! "Bring forth the royal diadem, and crown Him Lord of all." O blessed day of acclamations! How shall heaven's vault be rent with them when His saints shall see for themselves what was reserved for Him and for them in the "hereafter."

"Ye shall see the Son of man at the right hand of power, and coming in the clouds of heaven."

That word *hereafter* is, at this moment, our grandest comfort, and I wish to bring it before you in that light. Have you been misunderstood, misrepresented, slandered because of fidelity to the right and to the true? Do not trouble yourself. Vindicate not your own cause. Refer it to the King's throne above and say, "Hereafter, hereafter."

Have you been accused of being foolish, fanatical, and I know not what besides, because to you party is nothing and ecclesiastical pride nothing and the stamp of popular opinion nothing, because you are determined to follow the steps of your Master and believe the true and do the right? Then be in no hurry; the sure hereafter will settle the debate. Or are you very poor, and very sick and very sad? But are you Christ's own? Do you trust Him? Do you live in fellowship with Him? Then the hope of the hereafter may well take the sting out of the present.

It is not for long that you shall suffer; the glory will soon be revealed in you and around you. There are streets of gold symbolic of your future wealth, and there are harps celestial emblematic of your eternal joy. You shall have a white robe soon, and the dusty garments of toil shall be laid aside forever. You shall have a far more exceeding and an eternal weight of glory, and therefore the light affliction that is but for a moment may well be endured with patience.

Have you labored in vain? Have you tried to bring souls to Christ and had no recompense? Fret not, but remember the hereafter. Many a laborer, unsuccessful to the eye of man, will receive from his Master in that day a "Well done, thou good and faithful servant" (Matt. 25:21). Put little importance on anything you have and wish but lightly for anything that you have not. Let the present be to you, as it really is, a dream, an empty show, and project your soul into the hereafter, which is solid and enduring, for oh, what music there is in it!—what delight to a true child of God! "Nevertheless, hereafter."

Henceforward

Where am I to look for my third bell? Where is the third word I spoke of? In truth, I cannot find it in the version that we commonly use, and there is no third word in the original, and yet the word I am thinking of is there. The truth is that the second word, which has been rendered by *hereafter*, carries another meaning. I will give you what the Greek critics say, as nearly as can be, what the meaning of the word is—*henceforward*. "Henceforward ye shall see the Son of man sitting at the right hand of power, and coming in the clouds of heaven."

Henceforward. That is another word, and the teaching gathered out of it is this: *even in the present there are tokens of the victory of Christ.* "But," says one, "did Christ say to those priests that henceforward they should see Him sitting at the right hand of power?" Yes, yes, that is what He meant. He meant, "You look at Me and scorn Me; but, sirs, you shall not be able to do this any longer, for henceforward you shall see for yourselves that I am not what I appear to be, but that I sit at the right hand of power. Henceforward, and as long as you live, you shall know that galling truth."

And did that come true? Yes, it came true that night, for when the Savior died, there came a messenger to the members of the Sanhedrin and others who told them that the veil of the temple was rent in two. In that moment, when the Man of Nazareth died, that splendid piece of tapestry seemed to tear itself asunder from end to end as if in horror at the death of its Lord. The members of that council, when they met each other in the street and spoke of the news, must have been dumb in sheer astonishment; but while they looked upon each other, the earth they stood upon reeled and reeled again, and they could scarcely keep their feet. This was not the first wonder that had that day startled them, for the sun had been covered in unnatural darkness. At midday the sun had ceased to shine, and now the earth ceases to be stable.

Lo, also, in the darkness of the evening, certain members of this council saw the sheeted dead, newly risen from their sepulchers, walking through the streets, for the rocks rent, the earth shook, the graves opened, and the dead came forth and appeared to many. Thus, they began to know nearly immediately that the Man of Nazareth was at the right hand of power.

Early on the third morning, when they were met together, there came a messenger in hot haste who said, "The stone is rolled away from the door of the sepulcher. Remember that you placed a watch, and that you set your seal upon the stone. But early this morning the soldiers say that He came forth. He rose, that dreaded One whom we put to death, and at the sight of Him the keepers did quake and became as dead men."

Now, these members of the Sanhedrin believed that fact, and we have clear evidence that they did so, for they bribed the soldiers, and said, "Say ye, His disciples came by night, and stole him away while we slept" (Matt. 28:13). Then did the word also continue to be fulfilled, and they plainly saw that Jesus, whom they had condemned, was at the right hand of power. A few weeks passed over their heads, and there was a noise in the city and an extraordinary excitement. Peter had been preaching, and three thousand persons in one day had been baptized into the name that they dreaded so much; and they were told, and they heard it on the best of evidence, that there had been a wonderful manifestation of the Holy Spirit such as was spoken of in the book of the prophet Joel.

Then they must have looked one another in the face and stroked their beards and bitten their lips and said one to another, "Did He not say that we should see Him at the right hand of power?" They had often to remember that word and again and again to see its truth, for when Peter and John were brought before them, it was proven that they had restored a lame man, and these two unlearned and ignorant men told them that it was through the name of Jesus that the lame were made to leap and walk.

Day after day they were continuously obliged against their will to see, in the spread of the religion of the Man whom they had put to death, that His name had power about it such as they could not possibly refute or resist. One of their very own number, Paul, had been converted and was preaching the faith that he had endeavored to destroy. They must have been much amazed and chagrined, as in this also they discerned that the Son of Man was at the right hand of power.

Read the text as meaning, "Henceforward, ye shall see the Son of man at the right hand of power, and coming in the clouds of heaven." It is not the full meaning of the passage, but it is a part of that meaning, beyond all question.

Believer, even at the present time we may see the signs of the power of Christ among us. Only signs, mark you; I do not want to take you off from the hereafter, but even now there are tokens of the power of our Lord Jesus. Look at revivals. When they break out in the church, how they stagger all the adversaries of Christ. They dared to say that the gospel had lost all its power, that since the days of Whitefield and Wesley there was no hope of the masses being stirred, yet when they see, even in this church, from Sabbath to Sabbath, vast crowds listening to the Word, and when some few months ago no building was large enough to accommodate the thronging masses who sought to hear our American brethren, then were they smitten in the mouth so that they could speak no more, for it was manifested that the Lord Christ still lives and that, if His gospel is fully and simply preached, it will still draw all men to Him, and the souls will be saved, and, that not a few.

And look out into the brave world apart from religion, what influences there are abroad that are due to the power of the Christ of God. Would you have believed it twenty years ago that in America there should be no more a slave, that a united Italy should be free of her despots? No, the wonders of history, even within the past few years, are enough to show *us* that Christ is at the right hand of power. Come what will in the future, it will never be possible to uphold tyranny and oppression long, for the Lord Christ is to the front for the poor and needy of the earth.

O despots, you may do what you will and use your craft and policy if you please, but all over this world, the Lord Jesus Christ has set up a righteous standard, and He will draw a straight line, and it will pass through everything that offends, that it may be cut off. And it will also pass over all that is good and lovely and right and just and true, and these shall be established in His reign among men. I believe in the reign of Christ. Kings, sultans, czars—these are puppets, all of them, and your parliaments and congresses are but vanity of vanity. God is great, and none but He. Jesus is the King in all the earth. He is the Man, the King of men, the Lord of all. Glory be to His name.

As the years progress, we shall see it more and more, for He has had long patience, but He is beginning now to cut the work short in righteousness. He is baring His right arm for war, and that which denies manhood's just claims, that which treads upon the neck of the humanity that Christ has taken, that which stands against His throne and dominion must be broken in pieces like a potter's vessel, for the scepter in His hand is a rod of iron, and He will use it mightily. The Christ, then, gives signs still of His power. They are only tokens, but they are sure ones, even as the dawn does not deceive us, though it is not the noontide.

It will be a blessed thing if every reader, becoming a believer in Jesus, shall henceforward see Him at the right hand of power and coming in the clouds of heaven. Would to God we could live with that vision full in view, believing Jesus to be at the right hand of power, trusting Him and resting in Him. Because we know Him to be the Lord, strong and mighty, the Lord mighty in battle, we should never have a doubt when we are doing what is right. We should never have a doubt when we are following Jesus, for He is more than a conqueror, and so shall His followers be. Let us go on courageously, trusting in Him as a child trusts in his father, for He is mighty upon whom we rest our confidence.

Let us also keep before our mind's eye the fact that He is coming. Be not as the virgins that fell asleep. Even now my ear seems to hear the midnight cry, "Behold, the bridegroom cometh!" (Matt. 25:6). Arise, sleep no longer, for the Bridegroom is near.

As for you foolish virgins, God grant that there may yet be time enough left to awake even you, that you may yet have oil for your lamps before He comes. He comes we know not when, but He comes quickly. Be ready, for in such an hour as you think not the Son of Man comes. Be as men who watch for their Lord and as servants who are ready to give their account, because the master of the house is near.

You know I am not a prophet. I do not understand the visions of Daniel or Ezekiel. I find I have enough to do to teach the simple word such as I find in Matthew, Mark, Luke, and John, and the epistles of Paul. I do not find many souls have been converted to God by exquisite dissertations about the battle of Armageddon and all those other fine things. I have no doubt that prophesyings are very profitable, but I rather question whether they are so profitable to the hearers as they may be to the preachers and publishers. I believe that among a certain type of religious people, the futile explanations of prophecy issued by certain teachers gratify a craving that in irreligious people finds its food in novels and romances. People have a burning desire to know the future, and certain divines pander to this depraved taste by prophesying for them and letting them know what is coming by and by. I do not know the future, and I shall not pretend to know. But I do preach this, because I know it, that Christ will come, for He says so in a hundred passages.

Chapter Six

Citizenship in Heaven

For our conversation is in heaven; from whence also we look for the Saviour, the Lord Jesus Christ—Philippians 3:20.

JUST AS THERE CAN BE no comparison between a soaring seraph and a crawling worm, there should be no comparison between the lifestyles of Christians and the people of the world. It should be not a comparison but a contrast. No scale of degrees should be possible; the believer should be a direct and manifest contradiction to the unbeliever. The life of a saint should be altogether above and out of the same league as the life of a sinner. We should compel our critics not to confess that moralists are good and Christians a little better, but while the world is darkness, we should manifestly be light, and while "the whole world lieth in the wicked one" (1 John 5:19), we should most evidently be of God and overcome the temptations of that wicked one. As wide apart as the magnetic poles are life and death, light and darkness, health and disease, purity and sin, spiritual and carnal, divine and flesh. If we were what we profess to be, we should be as distinct a people in the midst of this world as a sheep from a goat or a lamb from a wolf.

Alas, the Church is so much adulterated that we have to decrease our glorying and cannot exalt her character as we would!

"The precious sons of Zion, comparable to fine gold, how are they esteemed as earthen pitchers, the work of the hands of the potter!" (Lam. 4:2). Oh, for the time when "our conversation is in heaven" and the base life of the man, "whose end is destruction, whose God is their belly" (Phil 3:19), shall be rebuked by our unworldly, unselfish character. The purity of our character should be such that men must acknowledge that we are of another and superior race.

Our text, I think, might be best translated: "Our citizenship is in heaven." The French translation renders it, "As for us, our burgess-ship is in the heavens." Doddridge paraphrases it, "But we converse as citizens of heaven, considering ourselves as denizens of the New Jerusalem, the only strangers and pilgrims upon earth."

We Are Strangers Here

The first idea that is suggested by the verse under consideration is this: If our citizenship is in heaven, we are strangers and foreigners, pilgrims and sojourners in the earth, as all our fathers were. "For here have we no continuing city," but we "desire a better country, that is, an heavenly" (Heb. 13:14; 11:16). Let us illustrate our position. A certain young man is sent to America by his father to trade on behalf of the family and is now living in New York. Being a citizen of England, though he lives in America and trades there, yet he is a foreigner and stands apart from the politics and afflictions of that nation. Yet he is subject to the laws and ways of the country that affords him shelter, and he must see to it that he does not fail to render it. A person trading in New York or Boston, though a freeman of the city of London, will find himself very much affected by the trade of the United States. When the merchants of his city suffer, he will find himself suffering with them. The fluctuations of their money market will affect his undertakings, and the recession of business will slow his progress; but if a healthy economy returns, he will find that as other businesses improve, his family's business interests will improve. He is not an American citizen, and yet every trembling of the scale will affect him; he will prosper as that nation prospers, and he will suffer as that nation suffers, that is to say, not as a citizen but as a trader.

And so we in this spiritual country find that though we are strangers and foreigners on earth, we share all the inconveniences of the flesh. No exemption is granted to us from the common lot of mankind. We are born to trouble, even as others, and have tribulation like the rest. When famine comes, we hunger; when war rages, we are in danger; we are exposed to the same climate, bearing the same burning heat or the same freezing cold; we know the whole range of afflictions, even as the citizens of earth know them. When God in mercy scatters liberally the bounties of His providence with both His hands, we take our share. Though we are foreigners, we live upon the good of the land and share the tender mercies of the God of providence. Thus, we have to take some interest in it; and the good man, though he is a foreigner, will not live even a week in this foreign land without *seeking to do good* among the neighbors with whom he dwells.

The good Samaritan sought the good not only of the Samaritan nation but also of the Jews. Though there was no true kinship among them (for the Samaritans were not, as we have often heard erroneously said, first cousins or relations to the Jews—not a drop of Jewish blood ran in the Samaritans' veins, for they were strangers brought from Assyria who had no relation to Abraham whatever), yet the good Samaritan, finding himself traveling between Jericho and Jerusalem, did good to the Jew, since he was in Judea. The Lord charged His people by His servant Jeremiah, "Seek the peace of the city whither I have caused you to be carried away captives, and pray unto the LORD for it: for in the peace thereof shall ye have peace" (Jer. 29:7). Since we are here, we must seek the good of this world. "But to do good and to communicate forget not" (Heb. 13:16). "But love ye your enemies, and do good, and lend, hoping for nothing again; and your reward shall be great, and ye shall be the children of the Highest: for he is kind unto the unthankful and to the evil" (Luke 6:35). We must do our utmost while we are here to bring men to Christ, to win them from their evil ways, to bring them to eternal life, and to make them, with us, citizens of another and a better land.

Seeking the good of the country as strangers and aliens, we must also remember that foreigners are obligated to *keep themselves very quiet*. What business do foreigners have in plotting against the government or intruding in the politics of a country in which they have no citizenship? So, in this land of ours, where you and I are strangers, we must be orderly sojourners, submitting ourselves constantly to those who are in authority, leading orderly and peaceable lives. According to the command of the Holy Ghost through the apostle, we must also "Honour all men. Love the brotherhood. Fear God. Honour the king" (1 Pet. 2:17). In addition, He says, "Submit yourselves to every ordinance of man for the Lord's sake" (1 Pet. 2:13). We are simply passing through this earth and should bless it in our transit but never yoke ourselves to its affairs. As *men*, Christians love liberty and are not willing to lose it even in the lower sense; but, spiritually, their politics are spiritual, and as citizens they look to the interest of that divine republic to which they belong, and they wait for the time when, having patiently borne with the laws of the land of their banishment, they shall come under the more beneficent sway of Him who reigns in glory, the King of kings and Lord of lords. If it is possible, as much as lies in you, live peaceably with all men and serve your generation still but never build your soul's dwelling place here, for all this earth must be destroyed at the coming of the fiery day.

Again, let us remember that as strangers *we have privileges as well as duties*. The princes of evil cannot draft us into their regiments; we cannot be compelled to do Satan's work. The king of this world may make his servants follow him, but he cannot raise a conscription from foreigners. He may order out his troops to this evil deed or that dastardly service, but the child of God claims an immunity from all the commands of Satan. Let evil maxims bind the men that are under their sway, but we are free and will not follow the prince of the power of the air. I know that men of this world say we must keep up appearances, we must be respectable, we must do as others do, we must swim with the tide, we must move with the crowd, but not so the true believer. "No," says the Christian. "Do not expect me to fall in with your ways and customs. Though I am in Rome, I shall not do as Rome does. I will let you see that I am a foreigner and that I have rights as a foreigner. Even in this alien land, I am not to be bound to fight your battles or march at the sound of your drums." We are soldiers of Christ, enlisted in *His* army, and as foreigners, we are not to be constrained into the army of evil. Be it known, O world, that we will not serve your gods or worship the image that you have set up. Servants of God we are, and we will not be in bondage to men or the things of this world.

As foreigners we are free from the conscription of the state, so we must remember also that we are *not eligible for its honors*. I know you will say that is not a privilege, but it is a great blessing if looked at correctly. While an Englishman in New York is not eligible for the office of the American president or the governor of Massachusetts, he may well be content to renounce both the difficulties and the honor of that office. So, also, the Christian is not eligible for this world's honors. It is a bad sign to hear the world clap its hands and say, "Well done," to the Christian man. That approval should cause the Christian to wonder whether he has not been doing wrong. "What did I do wrong," asked Socrates, "that yonder villain praised me just now?" And so the Christian must ask, "What have I done wrong, that so-and-so spoke well of me, for if I had done right he would not. He does not have the sense to praise goodness and applauds only that which suits his own taste." Never covet the world's esteem; the love of this world is not in keeping with the love of God. "If any man love the world, the love of the Father is not in him" (1 John 2:15). Treat its smiles as you treat its threats, with quiet contempt. Be willing rather to be sneered at than to be approved, counting the cross of Christ greater riches than all the treasures of Egypt. The men of this world will attempt to raise us to their seats of honor, for we are citizens of another country. Like the Trojans of old, we may be beguiled with presents even if unconquered in arms. Renounce then the grandeur and honor of this fleeting age. Pass through Vanity Fair without trading in its vanities; when they cry, "What will you buy?" answer only "We buy the truth."

Furthermore, as strangers, *it is not for us to hoard up this world's treasures*. If we are aliens, the treasures of this world are like bits of paper, of little value in our esteem, and we should lay up our treasure in heaven, "where neither moth nor rust doth corrupt, and where thieves do not break through nor steal" (Matt. 6:20). The money of this world is not circulating in Paradise, and when we reach its blissful shore, if regret can be known, we shall wish that we had laid up more treasure in the land of our fatherhood, in the dear fatherland beyond the skies.

Transport your jewels to a safer country than this world; be rich toward God rather than before men. While collecting funds for a chapel, a minister called upon a rich merchant, who generously gave him fifty pounds. As the minister was going out with sparkling eye at the liberality of the businessman, the merchant opened a letter and said, "Stop a minute, I find by this letter, I have lost a ship worth six thousand pounds." The poor minister trembled in his shoes, for he thought the next word would be, "Let me have the fifty-pound check back." Instead the merchant said, "Let me have the check back a moment," and then taking out his pen he wrote the minister a check for five hundred pounds. "As my money is going so fast, it is good," said he, "to make sure of some of it, so I will put some of it in God's bank." The minister went his way astonished at such a way of dealing as this, but indeed that is just what a man should do who feels that he is an alien here and his treasure is beyond the sky.

We Are Citizens in Heaven

What is meant by our being citizens in heaven? First that *we are under heaven's government*. Christ the king of heaven reigns in our hearts; the laws of glory are the laws of our consciences; our daily prayer is "Thy will be done in earth, as it is in heaven" (Matt. 5:10). The proclamations issued from the throne of glory are freely received by us; the decrees of the Great King we cheerfully obey. We are not without law to Christ. The Spirit of God rules in our mortal bodies, grace reigns through righteousness, and we wear the easy yoke of Jesus. Oh, that He would sit as king in our hearts, like Solomon upon his throne of gold! We are Yours, Jesus, and all that we have; rule us without a rival.

As citizens of the New Jerusalem, *we share heaven's honors*. The glory that belongs to beatified saints belongs to us, for we are already sons of God, already princes of royal blood; already we wear the spotless robe of Jesus' righteousness; already we have angels for our servitors, saints for our companions, Christ for our brother, God for our Father, and a crown of immortality for our reward. We share the honors of citizenship, for we have come to the general assembly and Church of the firstborn, whose names are written in heaven. "Beloved, now are we the sons of God, and it doth not yet appear what we shall be: but we know that, when he shall appear, we shall be like him; for we shall see him as he is" (1 John 3:2).

As citizens, *we have common rights in all the property of heaven*. The wide extensive plains of glory, the harps of gold and crowns of glory, the gates of pearl and walls of chrysolite, the azure light of the city that needs no candle or light of the sun, the river of the water of life, and the twelve manner of fruits that grow on the trees planted at the side are all ours. There is nothing in heaven that does not belong to us, for our citizenship is there. "Things present, or things to come; all are yours; and ye are Christ's; and Christ is God's" (1 Cor. 3:22–23).

And as we are thus under heaven's government, sharing its honors and partaking of its possessions, so we today *enjoy its delights.* Do they rejoice over sinners who are born to God—prodigals who have returned? So do we. Do they chant the glories of triumphant grace? We do the same. Do they cast their crowns at Jesus' feet? Such honors as we have, we cast there, too. Do they rejoice in Him? So also do we. Do they triumph, waiting for His second coming? By faith we triumph in the same. Are they singing "Worthy is the Lamb"? We also have sung the same tune, not to such glorious notes as theirs but with as sincere hearts; with minstrelsy not quite so splendid, but we hope as sincere, for the Spirit gave us the music that we have, and the Spirit gave them the thunders of their acclamations before the throne. "Our citizenship is in heaven."

We rejoice to know also that as the result of our being citizens, or rather I should say as the cause of it, our *names are written in the roll* of heaven's freemen. When at last the list shall be read, our names shall be read, too. Where Paul and Peter, where David and Jonathan, and where Abraham and Jacob shall be found, we shall be found, too. Numbered with them we were in the divine purpose, reckoned with them we were in the purchase on the cross, and with them shall we sit down forever at the tables of the blessed. The small and the great are fellow citizens and of the same household. The babes and the perfect men are recorded in the same great registry, and neither death nor hell can erase a single name.

Our citizenship, then, is in heaven. We do not have the space to extend that thought, but as John Calvin says of this text, "It is a most abundant source of many exhortations, which it were easy for any one to elicit from it." We are not all Calvins, but even to our smaller capacities, the subject appears to be one not easily exhausted but rich with unfathomable joy.

Our Conversation Is in Heaven

As citizens of heaven, our walk and actions must be consistent with the dignity of our position. Among the old Romans, when a dastardly action was proposed, it was thought a sufficient refusal to answer, "*Romanus sum*—I am a Roman." Surely it should be a strong incentive to every good thing if we can claim to be freemen of the Eternal City. Let our lives be conformed to the glory of our citizenship. In heaven they are holy, so must we be—so are we if our citizenship is not a mere pretense. They are happy, so must we be rejoicing in the Lord always. In heaven they are obedient, so must we be, following the faintest whispers of the divine will. In heaven they are active, so should we be, both day and night praising and serving God. In heaven they are peaceful, so should we find rest in Christ and be at peace even now. In heaven they rejoice to behold the face of Christ, so should we be always meditating upon Him, studying His beauties, and desiring to look into the truths that He taught. In heaven they are full of love, so should we love one another as brethren. In heaven they have sweet communion one with another, so should we, who though many are one body, be every one members one of the other. Before the throne they are free from envy, strife, jealousy, contention, falsehood, and anger, so should we be. We should, in fact, seek to so live by the manners and customs of the fatherland that others will say, "There goes a heavenly citizen, one who is with us, and among us, but is not of us."

Our very speech should be such that our citizenship is detected. We never live long in a house without men finding out what we are like. A friend of mine traveled to America and, landing at Boston, heard a man say, when somebody had dropped a cask on the pier, "Look out there, or else you will make a Coggeshall job of it." My friend said to him, "You are an Essex man, for that is a proverb used only in Essex: give me your hand," and they were friends at once. So there should be a ring of true metal about our speech and conversation so that when a brother meets us, he can say, "You are a Christian, I know, for only Christians speak or act like that." "Thou also wast with Jesus of Galilee,...for thy speech bewrayeth thee" (Matt. 26:69, 73). Our holiness should act as a sort of common calling by which we know how to give the right hand of fellowship to a stranger, who is not a real stranger but a fellow citizen with us and of the household of faith.

Dear friends, wherever we English wander, we should never forget our beloved land. In Australia or in the Cape of Good Hope or wherever else we may be exiled, surely every Englishman's eye must turn to this fair island; and with all her faults, we must love her still. And surely let us be where we may, our eyes must turn to heaven, the happy land unstained by shadow of fault. We love her still and love her more and more, praying for the time when our banishment shall expire and we shall enter into our fatherland to dwell there forever and ever.

Our Commerce Is in Heaven

The text says, "Our conversation is in heaven," and I think we may read it as though it said, "Our commerce is in heaven." We are trading on earth, but still the bulk of our trade is with heaven. We trade for trinkets in this land, but our gold and silver are in heaven. We commune with heaven, and how? Our trade is with heaven by *meditation*. We often think of God our Father and Christ our Brother, and by the Spirit, the Comforter, we are brought in contemplative delight to the general assembly and Church of the firstborn, whose names are written in heaven. Do not our *thoughts* sometimes burn within us when we trade with that blessed land. When I have sent the ships of understanding and consideration to that land of Ophir, which is full of gold, and they have come back again laden with all manner of precious things, my thoughts have been enriched, my soul has longed to journey to that good land. Black and stormy are you, O sea of death, but I would cross you to reach that land of Havilah, which has dust of gold. I know that anyone who is a Christian will never have his mind long off that better land.

And do you know we sometimes trade with heaven in our *hymns*? They say that when the Swiss soldiery is in foreign countries, there is a song that the band is forbidden to play because it reminds them of the cowbells of their native hills. If the men hear it, they are sure to desert, for that dear old song revives before their eyes the wooden chalets and the cows and the pastures of the glorious Alps, and they long to be away. There are some of our hymns that make us homesick, until we are hardly content to stop. I feel the spirit of Charles Wesley when he said—

> *O that we now might see our guide!*
> *O that the word were given!*
> *Come, Lord of hosts, the waves divide,*
> *And land us all in heaven.*

We trade with heaven, I hope, too, not only by meditation and by thought and by song but also *by hopes and by loves*. Our love is toward that land. How heartily the Germans sing of the dear old fatherland, but they cannot, with all their Germanic patriotism, beat the genial glow of the Briton's heart when he thinks of his fatherland. The Scot, too, wherever he may be, remembers the land of "brown heath and shaggy wood." And the Irishman, let him be where he will, still thinks the Emerald Isle the first gem of the sea. It is right that the patriot should love his country. Does not our love fervently flame toward heaven? We think we cannot speak well enough of it, and indeed here we are correct, for no exaggeration is possible. When we talk of that land of Eschol, our mouths are watering to taste its clusters; already, like David, we thirst to drink of the well that is within the gate; and we hunger after the good corn of the land. Our ears are wanting to be finished with the discords of earth that they may open to the harmonies of heaven, and our tongues are longing to sing the melodious sonnets sung by flaming ones above.

Just as people in a foreign land who love their country always are glad to have plenty of letters from the country, I hope we have much *communication with the old fatherland*. We send our prayers there as letters to our Father, and we get His letters back in the blessed volume of His Word. If you go into an Australian settler's hut and find a newspaper, where is it from? A gazette from the south of France? Oh no, it is a newspaper from England, addressed to him in his old mother's handwriting, bearing the postage stamp with the good Queen's face in the corner. And he likes it, though it is only a newspaper from some little country town with no noteworthy news in it, yet he likes it because it talks to him about the village where he lived and consequently touches a special string in the harp of his soul.

So must it be with heaven. This book, the Bible, is the newspaper of heaven, and therefore we must love it. The sermons that are preached are good news from a far country. The hymns we sing are notes by which we tell our Father of our welfare here and by which He whispers into our soul His continued love to us. I hope, too, we are sending a great many things home. I hope as we are strangers on earth, we are not laying up our treasure here, where we may lose it, but are packing it off as quickly as we can to our own country. There are many ways of doing it. God has many banks, and they are all safe ones. We have but to serve His Church or serve the souls that Christ has bought with His blood or help His poor, clothe His naked, and feed His hungry, and we send our treasures beyond the sea in a safe ship, and so we keep up our commerce with the skies.

Christ Is Coming

There is a great reason why we should live like aliens and foreigners here, and that is, Christ is coming soon. The early Church never forgot this. Did they not pant and thirst after the return of their ascended Lord? Like the twelve tribes, day and night they instantly watched for the Messiah. But the Church has grown weary of this hope. There have been so many false prophets who tell us that Christ is coming that the Church thinks He never will come, and she begins to deny or to keep in the background the blessed doctrine of the second advent of her Lord from heaven. I do not think the fact that there have been many false prophets should make us doubt our Lord's true word. Perhaps the very frequency of these mistakes may show that there is truth at the bottom. And so, though the false prophets have said, "Lo, here," and "Lo, there," and yet Christ has not come, that does not prove that His glorious appearing will never arrive.

You know I am not a prophet. I do not understand the visions of Daniel or Ezekiel. I find I have enough to do to teach the simple word such as I find in Matthew, Mark, Luke, and John, and the epistles of Paul. I do not find many souls have been converted to God by exquisite dissertations about the battle of Armageddon and all those other fine things. I have no doubt that prophesyings are very profitable, but I rather question whether they are so profitable to the hearers as they may be to the preachers and publishers. I believe that among a certain type of religious people, the futile explanations of prophecy issued by certain teachers gratify a craving that in irreligious people finds its food in novels and romances. People have a burning desire to know the future, and certain divines pander to this depraved taste by prophesying for them and letting them know what is coming by and by. I do not know the future, and I shall not pretend to know. But I do preach this, because I know it, that *Christ will come*, for He says so in a hundred passages.

The epistles of Paul are full of the advent of Christ, and Peter's, too, and John's letters are crowded with it. The best of saints have always lived on the hope of the advent. There was Enoch, who prophesied of the coming of the Son of Man. So there was another Enoch who was always talking of the coming, and saying, "Come quickly." I will not divide my readers by discussing whether the advent will be premillennial or postmillennial, or anything of that;

it is enough for me that *He will come*, and "in such an hour as ye think not the Son of man cometh" (Matt. 24:44). Tonight He may appear; just when we think that the thief will not come, he shall break open the house. We should therefore be always watching.

I think the Church would do well to be always living as if Christ might come today. Never mind about the meaning of the seven vials of Revelation. Fill your own vial with sweet odors and offer it before the Lord. Think what you like about Armageddon, but forget not to fight the good fight of faith. Guess not at the precise time for the destruction of the antichrist, but go and destroy it yourself, fighting against it every day, but be looking forward to and hastening the coming of the Son of Man. Let this be at once your comfort and excitement to diligence—that the Savior will soon come from heaven.

One of the sweetest thoughts I have ever known is that I shall meet my church members in heaven. There are so many in our church that I hardly get to shake hands with some but once in a year, but I shall have plenty of time in heaven. You will know your pastor in heaven better than you do now. He loves you now, and you love him. We shall then have more time to recount our experience of divine grace and praise God together and sing together and rejoice together concerning Him by whom we were helped to plant and sow and through whom all the increase came.

But we shall not all meet in glory, not all unless you repent. Some of you will certainly perish unless you believe in Christ. But why must we be divided? Oh, why not all in heaven! "Believe on the Lord Jesus Christ, and thou shalt be saved" (Acts 16:31). Trust Christ, and heaven is yours, and mine, and we are safe forever.

If you have been by grace enabled to live as you should, you have walked the separated path with Jesus; you have been in the world, but not of it, holy, harmless, undefiled, and separate from sinners. Therefore you have been despised; you have had to take your share of being unknown and misrepresented because you are even as He was in the world. "Therefore the world knoweth us not, because it knew him not" (1 John 3:1). As He was here to serve, you have been with Him as a servant; you have carried His yoke and counted it an easy load. You have been crucified to the world with Him: you know the meaning of His cross and delight to bear it after Him. You are dead to the world with Him and wish to be as one buried to it. You have already in your measure partaken of His resurrection and are living in newness of life. Your life story is still to be like the life story of your Lord, only painted in miniature. The more you watch the life of Christ, the more clearly you will see the life of a spiritual man depicted in it, and the more clearly will you see what the saints' future will be. You have been with Christ in life, and you will be with Him when you come to die. You will not die the expiatory death of Jesus, but you will die feeling that "it is finished," and you will breathe out your soul, saying, "Father, into thy hand I commend my spirit."

Chapter Seven

Forever With the Lord

Then we which are alive and remain shall be caught up together with them in the clouds, to meet the Lord in the air: and so shall we ever be with the Lord—1 Thessalonians 4:17.

WE KNOW THAT THESE WORDS are full of consolation, for the apostle says in the next verse, "Wherefore comfort one another with these words." The very words, it appears, were dictated by the Holy Spirit, the Comforter, to be repeated by the saints to each other with the view of removing sorrow from the minds of the distressed. The comfort is intended to give us hope in reference to those who have fallen asleep. Look over the list of those who have departed from you, to your utmost grief, and let the words of our text be a handkerchief for your tears. Sorrow not as those who are without hope, for they are with the Lord though they are not with you, and remember that the day is coming when you shall surely meet them where your Lord is the center of fellowship forever and ever. The separation will be very transient; the reunion will be everlasting.

These words are also intended to comfort the saints with regard to themselves, and I pray that they may be a cordial to any who are sick with fear, a matchless medicine to charm away the heartache from all believers. The fact that you bear about a dying body is very evident to some of you by your frequent and increasing sicknesses and pains, and this, it may be, is a real source of depression of spirit. You know that soon you must go the way whereby you shall not return; but be not dismayed, for you shall not go into a strange country alone and unattended. There is a friend who remains closer than a brother who will not fail you or forsake you; and, moreover, you are going home. Your Lord will be with you while you are departing, and then you will be ever with Him. Therefore, though sickness warn you of the near approach of death, be not in the least dismayed; though pain and weariness should make your heart and flesh fail, yet doubt not of your triumph through the Redeemer's blood, though it should sometimes make your flesh to tremble when you remember your many sins and the weakness of your faith. Be of good cheer, for your sins and weakness of faith will soon be removed far from you, and you shall be in His presence, where there is fullness of joy, and at His right hand, where there are pleasures forevermore.

Observe that the comfort that the apostle here presents to us may be partly derived from the fact of the resurrection but not chiefly, for he does not so much refer to the words "the dead in Christ shall rise" as to these last: "so shall we ever be with the Lord." It is a marvelous truth that you will rise again; it is a sweeter truth that you will be "ever with the Lord." There is some consolation also in the fact that we shall meet our departed brethren when we all shall be caught up together in the clouds to meet the Lord in the air. Blissful will be the general assembling of the redeemed, never again to be broken up; the joy of meeting, never to part again, is a sweet remedy for the bitterness of separation. There is great comfort in it, but the main stress of consolation does not lie even there. It is pleasant to think of the eternal fellowship of the godly above, but the best of all is the promised fellowship with our Lord.

A Continuance

I regard Paul's words as a continuance of our present spiritual state: "so shall we ever be with the Lord." To my mind, the apostle means that nothing shall prevent our continuing to be ever with the Lord. Death shall not separate us, nor the terrors of that tremendous day when the voice of the archangel and the trump of God shall be heard. By divine plan and arrangement, all shall be so ordained that "so shall we ever be with the Lord." By being caught up into the clouds, or in one way or another, our abiding in Christ shall remain unbroken. As we have received Christ Jesus the Lord, so shall we walk in Him, whether in life or in death.

I understand Paul to mean that we are with the Lord now and that nothing shall separate us from Him. Even now like Enoch we walk with God, and we shall not be deprived of divine communion. Our fear might be that in the future state something might happen that would become a dividing gulf between us and Christ, but the apostle assures us that it will not be so, there shall be such plans and methods used that "so shall we ever be with the Lord."

We are with the Lord *in this life* in a high spiritual sense. Have you not read in Colossians 3:3, "for ye are dead, and your life is hid with Christ in God"? Were you not "buried with him in baptism, wherein also ye are risen with him through the faith of the operation of God, who hath raised him from the dead" (Col. 2:12)? Do you not know what it is to be dead to the world in Christ, and to be living a secret life with Him? Are you not risen with Christ, and do you not understand in some measure what it is to be raised up together and made to sit together in the heavenlies in Christ Jesus? If you are not with Him, you are not a Christian at all, for the mark of the Christian is that he follows Christ. It is essential to salvation to be a sheep of Christ's fold, a partaker of Christ's life, a member of His mystical body, a branch of the spiritual vine. Separated from Him, we are spiritually dead. Jesus has said, "If a man abide not in me, he is cast forth as a branch, and is withered; and men gather them, and cast them into the fire, and they are burned" (John 15:6). Jesus is not far from any of His people. It is our privilege to follow Him wherever He goes, and His loving word to us is, "Abide in me, and I in you" (John 15:4). May He enable us to realize this. Sometimes this union is very sweetly apparent to ourselves; "We may know him that is true, and we are in him that is true" (1 John 5:20), and in consequence we feel an intense joy, even Christ's own joy fulfilled in us.

This companionship is, we trust, made manifest to others by its fruits. It should always be so: the life of the Christian should be manifestly a life with Christ. Men should take knowledge of us that we have been with Jesus and have learned of Him. They should see that there is something in us that could not have been there if it were not for the Son of God: a temper, a spirit, a way of life that could not have come by nature but must have been wrought in us through grace that has been received from Him in whom dwells a fullness of grace, even our Lord Jesus Christ.

We are with Him in this sense, too, that His unchanging love is always set upon us and our love, feeble though it sometimes may be, never quite dies out. In both senses, that challenge of the apostle Paul is true: "Who shall separate us from the love of Christ?" (Rom. 8:35). We can say, "I am my beloved's, and his desire is toward me" (Song of Sol. 7:10); and, on the other hand, we also testify, "My beloved is mine, and I am his" (Song of Sol. 2:16). He claims us, and we claim Him: He loves us, and we love Him. There is a union of heart between us. For us to live is Christ: we have no other aim.

Christ is with us by the continued indwelling of the Holy Spirit, who is with us and shall be in us forever. His anointing abides on us, and because of it we abide in Christ Jesus. He has sent us the Comforter to represent Himself, and through the divine Spirit He continues to be with us, and so even now we are ever with the Lord.

Our Lord has also promised to be with us whenever we are engaged in His work. That is a grand word of encouragement: "Lo, I am with you alway, even unto the end of the world" (Matt. 28:20). Think not, therefore, that it will be the first time of our being with Christ when we shall see Him in glory, for even now He manifests Himself to us as He does not to the world. Has He not often fulfilled His promise, "Where two or three are gathered together in my name, there am I in the midst of them" (Matt. 18:20)? We have heard the sound of our Master's feet behind us when we have been going on His errands. We have felt the touch of His hand when we have come to the forefront of the battle for His sake. We have known that He dwells in us by His Spirit and is with us by the power through which He has attended our work and the deeds that He has accomplished by the gospel that we have proclaimed. The Lord Jesus is with His Church in her tribulation for His name's sake, and He will ever be so, for He forsakes not His saints. "Fear not, I am with you," is as much a word of the Lord under the gospel as in Old Testament times.

But the time is coming when *we shall die*, unless the Lord shall descend from heaven with a shout meanwhile. Assuredly in the article of death we shall still be with the Lord. "Yea, though I walk through the valley of the shadow of death, I will fear no evil: for thou art with me; thy rod and thy staff they comfort me" (Ps. 23:4). This makes dying such a magnificent work to the people of God, for then especially is Jesus seen to be near. By death the saints escape from death, and henceforth it is no more death for them to die. When Jesus meets His saints, there seems no iron gate to pass through, but in a moment, they close their eyes on earth and open them in glory.

After death, we shall abide awhile in the separate, disembodied state, and we shall know as to our soul what it is to be still with the Lord; for what did the apostle say? "We are confident, I say, and willing rather to be absent from the body, and to be present with the Lord" (2 Cor. 5:8). The dying thief was to be that day with Christ in Paradise, and such shall be our lot as soon as our souls shall have passed out of this tenement of clay into that wondrous state of which we know so little.

And this body that shall fall asleep, though apparently it shall be destroyed, yet shall it not be so, but it shall only slumber awhile and then awake again and say, "When I awake, I am still with thee" (Ps. 139:18). Constantly death is described as sleeping in Jesus: that is the state of the saint's mortal frame through the interim between death and resurrection. The angels shall guard our bodies. All that is essential to complete the identity of our body shall be securely preserved so that the very seed that was put into the earth shall rise again in the beauty of effervescence that becomes it. All, I say, that is essential shall be preserved intact because it is still with Christ. It is a glorious doctrine that is stated in 1 Thessalonians 5:9–10: "For God hath not appointed us to wrath, but to obtain salvation by our Lord Jesus Christ, who died for us, that, whether we wake or sleep, we should live together with him."

In due time the last trumpet shall sound and *Christ shall come,* but the saints shall be with Him. The infinite providence has so arranged that Christ shall not come without His people, for "them also which sleep in Jesus will God bring with him" (1 Thess. 4:14). The saints shall be with Him in the second advent as they are now. Our souls shall hear the shout of victory and join in it. The voice of the archangel shall be heard by all His redeemed, and the trump of God shall be sounded in the hearing of every one of His beloved, for we shall be with Jesus all through that glorious transaction. Whatever the glory and splendor of His second coming, we shall be with Jesus in it. I am not going to give you glimpses of the revealed future or offer any suggestion as to the sublime history that is yet to be written, but most certainly there is to be a last general judgment, and then we shall be with Christ, assessors with Him at that day. Being ourselves first acquitted, we shall take our seat upon the judgment bench with Him. What says the Holy Ghost by the apostle? "Do ye not know that the saints shall judge the world?... Know ye not that we shall judge angels?" (1 Cor. 6:2–3). The fallen angels, to their shame, shall in part receive the verdict of their condemnation from the lips of men, and thus vengeance shall be taken upon them for all mischief they have done to the sons of men. Think of it: amidst the terror of the tremendous day, you shall be at ease, resting in the love of God and beholding the glory of Christ, and "so shall you ever be with the Lord."

There is, moreover, to be a reign of Christ. I cannot read the Scriptures without perceiving that there is to be a millennial reign, as I believe, upon the earth, and that there shall be new heavens and a new earth, wherein dwells righteousness. Well, whatever that reign is to be, we shall reign also. "And he that overcometh, and keepeth my works unto the end, to him will I give power over the nations: and he shall rule them with a rod of iron; as the vessels of a potter shall they be broken to shivers: even as I received of my Father" (Rev. 2:26–27). He shall reign, but it will be "before his ancients gloriously" (Isa. 24:23). We shall be partakers in the splendors of the latter days, whatever they may be, and "so shall we ever be with the Lord."

The particular incident of the text does not exhaust the words, but you may apply them to the whole story of God's children. From the first day of the spiritual birth of the Lord's immortals until they are received up into the seventh heaven to dwell with God, their history may be summed up in these words: "So shall we ever be with the Lord." Whether caught up into the clouds or here below on this poor afflicted earth, in Paradise or in the renovated earth, in the grave or in the glory, we shall ever be with the Lord. And when the end comes, and God alone shall reign, and the mediatorial kingdom shall cease, ages, ages, and ages shall revolve, but "so shall we ever be with the Lord."

> *Blessed state! beyond conception!*
> *Who its vast delights can tell?*
> *May it be my blissful portion,*
> *with my Savior there to dwell.*

A Great Advancement

"So shall we ever be with the Lord." Surely, this is an advancement upon this present state, for however spiritually mature we may be, and however in consequence thereof we may be very near to our Lord Jesus, still we know that while we are present in the body we are absent from the Lord. This life at its very best is still comparatively an absence from the Lord, but in the world to come, we shall be more perfectly at home. Now we cannot in the highest sense be with Christ, for we must, according to the apostle's expression, "depart, and to be with Christ; which is far better" (Phil. 1:23); but there we shall be forever beholding His face unveiled. Earth is not heaven, though the believer begins the heavenly life while he is upon it. We are not with Christ as to place nor as to actual sight, but in the glory land, we shall be.

It is an advancement upon the present state of those who have died, for though their souls are with the Lord, their bodies are subject to corruption. Still does the sepulcher contain the blessed dust of the fathers of our Israel, or scattered to the four winds of heaven, the martyr's ashes are with us still. The glorified saints are not as yet consciously "with the Lord" as to their complete manhood, but when the grand event shall occur of which Paul speaks, the body shall be reanimated. This is our glorious hope. We can say with the patriarch Job, "For I know that my redeemer liveth, and that he shall stand at the latter day upon the earth: and though after my skin worms destroy this body, yet in my flesh shall I see God: whom I shall see for myself, and mine eyes shall behold, and not another; though my reins be consumed within me" (Job 19:25–27). Know you not, asked the apostle Paul, "that flesh and blood cannot inherit the kingdom of God?" (1 Cor. 15:50). That is, as we are: but "this corruptible must put on incorruption, and this mortal must put on immortality" (1 Cor. 15:53), and then shall the entire manhood, the perfected manhood, the fully developed manhood, of which this manhood is as it were but a shriveled seed, be in the fullest and divinest sense forever with the Lord. This is an advancement even upon the present state of departed saints in Paradise.

And now let us consider what this glorious condition is to which we shall be advanced. We shall be with the Lord in the strongest possible meaning of that language. So with Him that we shall never mind earthly things again, shall have no desire to go into the marketplace or into the office or into the field. We shall have nothing to do but to be engaged forever with Him in such occupations as shall have no tendency to take us off from communion with Him. We shall be so with Him as to have no sin to cloud our view of Him: the understanding will be delivered from all the injury that sin has done to it, and we shall know Him even as we are known. We shall see Him as a familiar friend and sit with Him at His marriage feast. We shall be with Him so as to have no fear of His ever being grieved and hiding His face from us again. We shall never again be made to cry out in bitterness of spirit, "Oh that I knew where I might find him!" (Job 23:3). We shall always know His love, always return it, and always swim in the full stream of it, enjoying it to the full.

There will be no lukewarmness to mar our fellowship. He shall never have to say to us, "I would thou wert cold or hot" (Rev. 3:15). There shall be no weariness to suspend our ceaseless bliss: we shall never have to cease from fellowship with Him, because our physical frame is exhausted through the excessive joy of our heart; the vessel will be strengthened to hold the new wine. No doubts shall intrude into our rest, neither doctrinal doubts nor doubts about our interest in Him, for we shall be so consciously with Him as to have risen ten thousand leagues above that gloomy state. We shall know that He is ours, for His left hand shall be under our head and His right hand shall embrace us, and we shall be with Him beyond all hazard of any removal from Him. Speak you of a thousand years of reigning? What is that compared with "forever with the Lord"? The millennium is little compared with "forever"—a millennium of millenniums would be nothing to it. There can come no end to us and no end to our bliss, since there can be no end to Him— "because I live, ye shall live also" (John 14:19).

"Forever with the Lord." What will it mean? One preacher stated it: "Forever life, forever light, forever love, forever peace, forever rest, forever joy." What a chain of delights! What more can heart imagine or hope desire? Carry those things in your mind and you will get, if you drink from them, some idea of the blessedness that is contained in being forever with the Lord; but still recollect these are only the fruits and not the root of the joy. Jesus is better than all these. His company is more than the joy that comes out of it. I do not care so much for "life forever" nor for "light forever" as I do with "forever with the Lord." Oh, to be with Him. I ask no other bliss and cannot imagine anything more heavenly.

We love to think of being with Jesus under the aspect that the text specially suggests to us. We are to be forever with the Redeemer, not as Jesus the Savior only but as *the Lord*. Here we have seen Him on the cross and lived thereby; we are with Him now in His cross bearing and shame, and it is well; but our eternal companionship with Him will enable us to rejoice in Him *as the Lord*. What did our Master say in His blessed prayer? "Father, I will that they also, whom thou hast given me, be with me where I am; that they may behold my glory" (John 17:24). It will be heaven to us to be forever with Him as the Lord. Oh, how we shall delight to obey Him as our Lord! How we shall triumph as we see what a lord He is over all the universe and what a conqueror He is over all His enemies! He will be more and more the Lord to us as we see all things put under Him. We shall forever hail Him as King of kings and Lord of lords. How we will adore Him there when we see Him in His glory. We do worship Him now and are not ashamed to believe that the Man of Nazareth is "very God of very God," but oh, how His deity will shine upon us with infinite brilliance when we come to be near Him. Thanks be to His name, we shall be strengthened to endure the sight, and we shall rejoice to see ourselves in the full blaze of His glory.

A Coherence

Those who are acquainted with the Greek language know that the *with* here is not *meta*, which signifies being in the same place with a person, but is *sun*, which goes very much further and implies a coherence—the two who are with each other are intimately connected. Let me show you what this means. We are to be forever with the Lord. The Christian's life is all along like the life of his Lord, and so it is a life with Christ. Jesus was in all things with His brethren, and grace makes us to be with Him.

Just quickly consider your spiritual experience and your Lord's life, and see the parallel. When you were newborn as a Christian, you were born as Jesus Christ was, for you were born of the Holy Spirit. What happened after that? The devil tried to destroy the new life in you, just as Herod tried to kill your Lord: you were with Christ in danger, early and imminent. You grew in stature and in grace, and while yet grace was young, you staggered those who were about you with the things you said and did and felt, for they could not understand you, even as when He went up to the temple, our Lord amazed the doctors who gathered around Him. The Spirit of God rested upon you, not in the same measure, but still, as a matter of fact, it did descend upon you as it did upon your Lord. You have been with Him in Jordan's stream and have received the divine acknowledgment that you are indeed the son of God. Your Lord was led into the wilderness to be tempted, and you too have been tempted of the devil. You have been with the Lord all along from the first day until now.

If you have been by grace enabled to live as you should, you have walked the separated path with Jesus; you have been in the world, but not of it, holy, harmless, undefiled, and separate from sinners. Therefore you have been despised; you have had to take your share of being unknown and misrepresented because you are even as He was in the world. "Therefore the world knoweth us not, because it knew him not" (1 John 3:1). As He was here to serve, you have been with Him as a servant; you have carried His yoke and counted it an easy load. You have been crucified to the world with Him: you know the meaning of His cross and delight to bear it after Him. You are dead to the world with Him and wish to be as one buried to it. You have already in your measure partaken of His resurrection and are living in newness of life. Your life story is still to be like the life story of your Lord, only painted in miniature. The more you watch the life of Christ, the more clearly you will see the life of a spiritual man depicted in it, and the more clearly will you see what the saints' future will be. You have been with Christ in life, and you will be with Him when you come to die. You will not die the expiatory death of Jesus, but you will die feeling that "it is finished," and you will breathe out your soul, saying, "Father, into thy hand I commend my spirit."

Think then, beloved, we are to be like Christ as to our character: we are to be with the Lord by sharing His moral and spiritual likeness. Conformed to His image, we shall be adorned with His beauty. Our Lord looks on His beloved as one with Himself and makes them like Himself. You remember how John bowed down before an angel in heaven (Rev. 22:8). It was a great blunder to make, but I dare say you and I will be likely to make the same, for the saints are so like their Lord. Recall the wonderful words: "we shall be like him; for we shall see him as he is" (1 John 3:2). Christ will rejoice to see the saints all covered with the glory that His Father has given Him. He will not be ashamed to call them brethren. Those poor people of His who were so full of weaknesses and mourned over it so much shall be so like Him that they shall be at once seen to be His brethren.

We shall be with Him in the sense that we shall be partakers of all the blessedness and glory that our adorable Lord now enjoys. We shall be accepted together with Him. Is He the beloved of the Lord? Does His Father's heart delight in Him, as well it may? Behold, you also shall be called Hephzibah, for "the LORD delighteth in thee" (Isa. 62:4). You shall be beloved of the Father's soul. Is He enriched with all manner of blessings beyond imagination? So shall you be, for He has blessed us with all spiritual blessings in Christ Jesus, according as He has chosen us in Him. Is Christ exalted? How loftily is He lifted up to sit upon a glorious high throne forever! But you shall sit upon His throne with Him and share His exaltation as you have shared His humiliation. Oh, the delight of thus being joint heirs with Christ and with Him in the possession of all that He possesses.

What is heaven? It is the place that His love suggested, that His genius invented, that His bounty provided, that His royalty has adorned, that His wisdom has prepared, that He Himself glorifies; in that heaven you are to be with Him forever. You shall dwell in the King's own palace. Its gates of pearl and streets of gold shall not be too good for you. You who love Him are to abide forever with Him—not near Him in a secondary place, as a servant lives at the lodge gate of His master's mansion, but with Him in the self-same palace in the metropolis of the universe.

In a word, believers are to be identified with Christ forever. That seems to me to be the very life and essence of the text: with Him forever, that is, identified with Him forever. Do they ask for the Shepherd? They cannot behold Him to perfection except as surrounded by His sheep. Will the King be illustrious? How can that be if His subjects are lost? Do they ask for the bridegroom? They cannot imagine Him in the fullness of joy without His bride. Will the Head be blessed? It could not be if it were separated from the members. Will Christ be forever glorified? How can He be if He shall lose His jewels? He is a foundation, and what would He be if all His people were not built upon Him into the likeness of a palace? O brethren, there shall be no Christ without Christians; there shall be no Savior without the saved ones; there shall be no Elder Brother without the younger brethren; there shall be no

Redeemer without His redeemed. We are His fullness, and He must have us with Him. We are identified with Him forever. Nothing can ever divide us from Him.

Two or three practical sentences. One word is this—*this "with the Lord" must begin now.* Do you wish to be forever with the Lord? You must be with Him by becoming His disciple in this life. None come to be with the Lord hereafter who are not with the Lord here in time.

Next, every Christian should seek to be more and more with Christ, for *the growth and glory of your life lie there.* Do you want to have heaven below? Be with Christ below. Do you want to know at once what eternal bliss is? Know it by living now with the Lord.

The next word is, *how plainly, then, the way of life is to be with the Lord.* If you want to be saved, you must be "with the Lord." There is no other way for you. Come near to Him and lay hold upon Him by faith. Life lies there. Come to Him by a humble, tearful faith. Come at once.

And finally, *what must it be to be without the Lord?* What must it be to be against the Lord? For it comes to this: "He that is not with me is against me" (Matt. 12:30). To be forever without the Lord, banished from His love and light and life and peace and rest and joy! What a loss will this be! What must it be to be forever against the Lord! Think of it: forever hating Jesus, forever plotting against Him, forever gnashing your teeth against Him; this is hell, this is the infinite of misery, to be against the Lord of love and life and light. Turn from this fatal course. Believe on Him: "Kiss the Son, lest he be angry, and ye perish from the way, when his wrath is kindled but a little. Blessed are all they that put their trust in him" (Ps. 2:12).

*T*o the true Christian, Christ is the object of his life. As the ship speeds toward the port, so the believer hastes toward the haven of his Savior's heart. As flies the arrow to its goal, so flies the Christian toward the perfecting of his fellowship with Christ Jesus. As the soldier fights for his captain and is crowned in his captain's victory, so the believer contends for Christ and gets his triumph out of the triumphs of his Master. "For to me to live is Christ" (Phil. 1:21); at least, it is this he seeks after and counts that all life apart from this is merely death in another form. That wicked flesh of his, those many temptations, that Satanic trinity of the world, the flesh, and the devil—all these mar the believer's outward actions. But if he could be what he would be, he would stand like the bullock at Christ's altar to be slaughtered or march forward like a bullock in Christ's furrow to plow the blood-bought field. He desires that he may not have a hair of his head unconsecrated or take one breath that is not for his Savior or speak one word that is not for the glory of his Lord. His heart's ambition is to live so long as he can glorify Christ better on earth than in heaven and to be taken up when it shall be better for him and more honorable for his Master that he should be with Jesus where He is. As the river seeks the sea, so, Jesus, I seek You! Let me find You and melt my life into Yours forever!

Chapter Eight

Christ Our Life—Soon to Appear

When Christ, who is our life, shall appear, then shall ye also appear with him in glory—Colossians 3:4.

OVER THE PAST FEW DAYS, I have wandered through a wilderness and traversed the valley of the shadow of death, but I will not repeat the howlings of Apollyon. I find that I must remember the ancient minstrel who, when the genius of song had for a time departed from him, was nevertheless called upon to play sweet music. What could he do but lay his fingers among the strings of his harp and begin some old familiar strain. His fingers and his lips moved at first mechanically; the first few stanzas dropped from him from mere force of habit and fell like stones without life or power. But by and by, he struck a string that woke the echoes of his soul; a note fell on his heart like a blazing torch, and the smoldering fire within his soul suddenly flamed up. The heaven-born muse was with him, and he sang as in his better times.

So I place my fingers on the strings that know so well the name of Jesus and take up a theme that so constantly has made the walls of my church to ring. I trust that despite my weariness of heart, these words shall nevertheless lead to something that may kindle in you hope and joy and love, if not rapture and delight. Oh, for the wings of eagles to bear our souls upward toward the throne of our God! Already my heart warms with the expectation of a blessing! Does the earth feel the rising of the sun before the first bright beams gild the east? Are there not sharp-witted birds that know within themselves that the sunbeams are on the road and therefore begin right joyously to wake up their fellows to tell them that the morning comes leaping over the hills? Certain hopeful, joyful thoughts have entered within our heart, prophetic of the Comforter's divine appearing, to make glad our souls. Believer, you shall once again behold Christ's comfortable presence; you shall no longer cry to Him out of the depths, but your soul shall lean upon His arm and drink deep of His love. Beloved, I proceed in the hope that the gracious Lord will favor His most unworthy servant and in His own mercy fulfill our best expectations.

Paul's word is a very simple one and bears upon its surface four thoughts: that *Christ is our life*, that, *Christ is hidden, and so is our life*, that, *Christ will one day appear*, and, that *when He appears we also shall appear with Him in glory*.

Christ Who Is Our Life

We hardly realize that we are reading in Colossians when we meet with this marvelously rich expression. It is so like John's way of talking. See John's opening words in his gospel: "In him was life; and the life was the light of men" (1:4). Remember how he reports the words at Lazarus' tomb: "I am the resurrection, and the life" (John 11:25). How familiarly John speaks of the Lord Jesus under the same character in the first verses of his first epistle: "That which was from the beginning, which we have heard, which we have seen with our eyes, which we have looked upon, and our hands have handled, of the Word of life; (for the life was manifested, and we have seen it, and bear witness, and shew unto you that eternal life which was with the Father, and was manifested unto us)." How close John clings to Jesus! He does not say as I do that Christ is the food of our life and the joy of our life and the object of our life, and so on; no, but "Christ *is* our life." I think that Peter or James would have said, "He is the *strength* or guide of our life," but John must put his head right into the Savior's bosom. John cannot talk at a distance or whisper from a second seat, but he must feel himself in the closest, nearest possible contact with his Lord, and so he puts it, "The life was manifested," getting to the very heart of it at once.

Paul has somewhat of the same loving spirit, and even though he may not have been entitled to be called that disciple "whom Jesus loved" (John 13:23), the angel might well have addressed him as he did Daniel: "O man greatly beloved" (Dan. 10:19). Hence, you see, Paul leaps at once into the depths of the truth and delights to dive in it. Whereas others, like the Israelites, stand outside the bound that surrounds the mount, he, like Moses, enters into the place where God is and beholds the excellent glory. We, I fear, must circle this holy truth before we can fully enter into it. Blessed is it to wait at the doors of such a truth, though better far to enter in. Let it be understood that it is not natural but spiritual life of which the text treats, and then we shall not mislead the ignorant.

Christ is the source of our life. "For as the Father raiseth up the dead, and quickeneth them; even so the Son quickeneth whom he will" (John 5:21). Our Lord's own words are "Verily, verily, I say unto you, He that heareth my word, and believeth on him that sent me, hath everlasting life, and shall not come into condemnation; but is passed from death unto life. Verily, verily, I say unto you, The hour is coming, and now is, when the dead shall hear the voice of the Son of God: and they that hear shall live" (John 5:24–25). Four *verilies*, as if to show the importance of the truth here taught to us. We are dead in sin. That same voice that brought Lazarus out of the tomb brings us out of our grave of sin. We hear the Word of God, and we live according to the promise: "Awake thou that sleepest, and arise from the dead, and Christ shall give thee light" (Eph. 5: 14). Jesus is our Alpha as well as our Omega; He is the Author of our faith as well as its finisher. We should have been to this day dead in trespasses and sins if it had not been said, "And you hath he quickened" (Eph. 2:1). It is by *His* life that we live; He gives us the living water that is in us a well of water springing up to everlasting life.

Christ is the substance of our spiritual life. What is life? The physician cannot discover it; the anatomist hunts in vain for it through flesh and nerve and brain. Be quick, sir, with that scalpel of yours when men say, "Life's just departed." Cut quick to the heart and see whether you cannot find at least some lingering footprint of the departed thing called life. Subtle anatomist, what have you found? Look at that brain—what can you see there but a certain quantity of matter strangely fashioned? Can you discover what is life? It is true that somewhere in that brain and in that spinal cord it dwells, and that heart with its perpetual pumpings and heavings has something or other to do with it, but where is the substance, the real substance of the thing called life? Ariel's wings cannot pursue it—it is too subtle. Thought knows it but cannot grasp it; knows it from its being like itself but cannot give a picture of it or represent what it is.

In the new nature of the Christian there is much mystery, but there is none as to what is its life. If you could cut into the center of the renewed heart, you would find sure footprints of divine life, for you would find love for Jesus, nay, you would find Christ Himself there. If you walk in search of the springs of the sea of the new nature, you will find the Lord Jesus at the fount of all. "All my springs are in thee," said David (Ps. 87:7). Christ creates the life throbs of the believer's soul; He sends the life floods through the man according to His own will. If you could penetrate the brain of the believer, you would find Christ to be the central thought moving every other thought and causing every other thought to take root and grow out of itself. You would find Christ to be the true substance of the inner life of the spiritual nature of every soul made alive by the breath of heaven's life.

Christ is the sustenance of our life. What can the Christian feed upon but Jesus' flesh and blood? As to his natural life, he needs bread, but as to his spiritual life, of which alone we are now speaking, he has learned that "man shall not live by bread alone, but by every word that proceedeth out of the mouth of God" (Matt. 4:4). "This is the bread which cometh down from heaven, that a man may eat thereof, and not die. I am the living bread which came down from heaven: if any man eat of this bread, he shall live for ever: and the bread that I will give is my flesh, which I will give for the life of the world" (John 6:50–51). We cannot live on the sand of the wilderness; we want the manna that drops from on high. Our skin bottles of creature confidence cannot yield us a drop of moisture, but we drink of the rock that follows us, and that rock is Christ.

O wayworn pilgrims in this wilderness of sin, you never do get a morsel, much less a meal, to satisfy the craving hunger of your spirits, except you find it in Christ Jesus. When you feed on Him, your soul can sing, "[He] satisfieth my mouth with good things; so that [my] youth is renewed like the eagle's" (Ps. 103:5). But if you do not have Jesus, your bursting wine vat and your well-filled barn can give you no sort of satisfaction; rather you lament over them in the words of wisdom: "Vanity of vanities, saith the preacher; all is vanity!" (Eccl. 12:8). How true are Jesus' own words: "For my flesh is meat indeed, and my blood is drink indeed. He that eateth my flesh, and drinketh my blood, dwelleth in me, and I in him. As the living Father hath sent me, and I live by the Father: so he that eateth me, even he shall live by me" (John 6:55–57).

Christ is the solace of our life. Noah's ark had but one window, and we must not expect more. Jesus is the only window that lets light into the Christian's spirit when he is under sharp affliction. A painting of a mariner's midnight voyage, when one star alone of all the heavenly host could guide his foundering ship to the port of peace, is a faint but truthful representation of the Christian's life in its hour of peril. Paul says that during his disastrous voyage "neither sun nor stars in many days appeared, and no small tempest lay on us, all hope that we should be saved was then taken away.... For there stood by me this night the angel of God, whose I am, and whom I serve, saying, Fear not, Paul" (Acts 27:20, 23–24). Even so will the Lord Jesus appear to His saints in their most difficult moments and be their joy and safety. And if Christ appears, what does it matter where we are?

Do not talk of poverty! Our tents are the curtains of Solomon and not the smoke-dried skins of Kedar when Christ is present. Speak not of your needs! There are all manner of precious fruits laid up for beloved ones when He comes to us. Speak not of sickness! My soul is no longer sick except it be of love, but full of holy health when once the sun of righteousness has risen with healing beneath His wings. Christ is the very soul of my soul's life. His loving kindness is better than life! There is nothing in life worth living for but Christ. "Whom have I in heaven but thee? and there is none upon earth that I desire beside thee" (Ps. 73:25). Christ is the golden grain, the only thing worth having. Life's true life, the true heart's blood, the innermost fount of life is in Jesus.

To the true Christian, *Christ is the object of his life.* As the ship speeds toward the port, so the believer hastes toward the haven of his Savior's heart. As flies the arrow to its goal, so flies the Christian toward the perfecting of his fellowship with Christ Jesus. As the soldier fights for his captain and is crowned in his captain's victory, so the believer contends for Christ and gets his triumph out of the triumphs of his Master. "For to me to live is Christ" (Phil. 1:21); at least, it is this he seeks after and counts that all life apart from this is merely death in another form. That wicked flesh of his, those many temptations, that Satanic trinity of the world, the flesh, and the devil—all these mar the believer's outward actions. But if he could be what he would be, he would stand like the bullock at Christ's altar to be slaughtered or march forward like a bullock in Christ's furrow to plow the blood-bought field. He desires that he may not have a hair of his head unconsecrated or take one breath that is not for his Savior or speak one word that is not for the glory of his Lord. His heart's ambition is to live so long as he can glorify Christ better on earth than in heaven and to be taken up when it shall be better for him and more honorable for his Master that he should be with Jesus where He is. As the river seeks the sea, so, Jesus, I seek You! Let me find You and melt my life into Yours forever!

It follows from all this that *Christ is the pattern of our life*. A Christian lays the life of Christ before him as the schoolboy puts his copy at the top of the page and tries to draw each line, downstroke and upstroke, according to the handwriting of Christ Jesus. He has the portrait of Christ before him as the artist has in his studio his Greek sculptures, busts, and torsos; he knows that there is all the true anatomy of virtue in Christ. If he wants to study life, he studies from Christ, or if he would closely learn the beauties of the ancients, he studies from the Savior, for Christ is ancient and modern, antique and living too, and therefore God's artists in their life-sculpture keep to the Savior and count that if they imitate every vein and sketch out every muscle of their great copy, they shall then have produced the perfection of manhood.

I would give nothing for your religion if you do not seek to be like Jesus Christ. Where there is the same life within, there will, there must be, to a great extent, the same developments without. I have heard it said, and I think I have sometimes noticed it, that husbands and wives who are truly knit together grow somewhat like each other in expression, if not in feature. This I well know, that if the heart is truly wedded to the Lord Jesus and lives in near fellowship with Him, it must grow like Him. Grace is the light, our loving heart is the sensitive film, Jesus is the person who fills the lens of our soul, and soon a heavenly photograph of His character is produced. There will be a similarity of spirit, temper, motive, and action; it will not be manifest merely in great things but in little matters, too, for even our speech will betray us.

I must pause a minute here just to say that what is true concerning our spiritual life *now* is *equally true of our spiritual life in heaven*. Different as are the circumstances of the life in heaven and the life on earth, yet as to real essence there is only one life in both places. Saints in heaven live by precisely the same life that makes them live here. Spiritual life in the kingdom of grace and in the kingdom of glory is the same, only here it is developing spiritual life, there it is perfect; here it is that of a babe, there it is fully manifested perfection; but in very deed the life is precisely the same. You who have been born again have now within you the life that will last on throughout eternity; you have the very same vital spark of heavenly flame that will burn in glory, world without end.

It will be no digression if we here remark that as we have eternal life in having Christ, this *marks our dignity.* "Christ our life!" Why, this cannot be said of princes or kings! What is their life? Talk of blue blood and pedigree, and so on, here is something more, here is *God's own Son, our life!* You cannot say this of angels. Bright spirits, your songs are sweet and your lives are happy, but Christ is not your life! Nay, this cannot be asserted of archangels. Gabriel, you may bend yourself before God's throne and worship Him in praise too high for me, but you cannot boast what I can surely claim, that Christ is my life! Herein men rise to a supernatural height, for they can say what no spirits but those redeemed by blood may venture to assert: "Christ is our life." Does not this account for *Christian holiness*? How can a man live in sin if Christ is his life? Jesus dwell in him and he continue in sin? Impossible! Can he sin without his life? He *must* do so if he sins, because Christ cannot sin, and Christ is his life. Why, if I see the saint never so self-denying, never so zealous, never so sincere, never so like his Lord, it is no wonder now, when I understand that Christ is his life.

See *how secure* the Christian is. No temptation, no hellish blast, no exhalation from the Stygian pits of temptation can ever with burning fever or chill disease waste the life of the Christian spiritually. No, it is hid with Christ, it *is* Christ, and unless Christ dies, the Christian's life does not. Oh, how safe, how honored how happy is the Christian!

Our Life Is Hidden in Christ

"For the earnest expectation of the creature waiteth for the manifestation of the sons of God" (Rom. 8:19), but as yet they are unknown and unmanifested. The major part of the believer's life is not seen at all and never can be by the unspiritual eye. Where is

Christ? The unbeliever says of Christ, "I cannot see Him, touch Him, hear Him. He is beyond all cognizance of my senses; therefore I do not believe in Him." Such is spiritual life to the unbeliever. You must not expect because you are a Christian that unbelievers will begin to admire you and say, "What a mystery! This man has a new life in him, what an admirable thing, what a desirable possession, we wish we partook of the same." Nothing of the kind. Unbelievers do not know that you have such a life at all. They can see your outward actions, but your inward life is quite out of reach of their observation. Christ is in heaven today; He is full of joy, but the world does not know His joy; no worldly heart is boasting and rejoicing because Christ is glad in heaven. Christ today is pleading before the Father's throne, but the world does not see Christ's petitioning; Christ's occupations are all hidden from carnal eyes. Christ at this present moment reigns and has power in heaven and earth and hell, but what does the worldly man see of it? Jesus has fellowship with all His saints everywhere, but what does the ungodly man discern?

I might stand and preach until midnight concerning my Lord, but all that men who are unconverted would gain would be to hear what I have to tell and then to say, "Perhaps it is true." But they could not possibly discern it, the thing is beyond the cognizance of sense. So is our spiritual life. Beloved, you may reign over sin, but the sinner does not comprehend your being a king. You may officiate as a priest before God, but the ungodly man does not perceive your priesthood and your worship. Do not expect him to do so; your labor is lost if you try by any way to introduce him to these mysteries except by the same door through which you came yourself.

I never try to teach a horse astronomy, and to teach an unconverted man spiritual experience would be a folly of the same sort. The man who knows nothing of our inner life takes up Bunyan's *Pilgrim's Progress* and says, "Yes, it is a very wonderful allegory." It is, sir, but unrenewed minds know nothing about it. When we have sometimes read explanations of the pilgrim's progress, we could not but detect that the writer had need to have had it explained to him; he could describe the shell, but the kernel of the nut was far beyond his reach. It must be so if Christ is our life; Christ has gone away and cannot be seen; it must be so that the greater proportion of the spiritual life must be forever a secret to all but spiritual men.

But then there is a part that men do see, and that I may liken to Christ when He was on earth: Christ seen of men and angels. What did the world do with Christ as soon as they saw Him? Set Him in the chair of state and fall down and worship His absolute perfection? No, not they: "He [was] despised and rejected of men; a man of sorrows, and acquainted with grief" (Isa. 53:3). Outside of the camp was His place; bearing the cross was for Him the occupation, not of one day but of every day. Did the world yield Him solace and rest? Foxes, you have your holes; you birds of the air, you have your nests; but the Son of Man had nowhere to lay His head. Earth could afford Him no bed, no house, no shelter; at last it cast Him out for death and crucified Him and then would have denied Him a tomb if one of His disciples had not begged His body. Such you must expect to be what is in store for the part of your spiritual life that men can see; as soon as they see it to be spiritual life, they will treat it as they treated the Savior. They will despise it. "Sure!" say they, "pretty conceptions, fine expressions, nice ideas." You expect them to give you comfort, do you?

Do you think that Christ would have anywhere to lay His head in this world today any more than He had two thousand years ago? You look around to find what God gives the foxes and the birds, but what He never meant to give to you in this world, a place whereon to lay your head. Your place to lay your head is upon your Savior's bosom, but not here. You dream that men will admire you, that the more holy you are and the more Christlike you are, the more peaceable people will be toward you. You do not know what you are driving at. "It is enough for the disciple that he be as his master, and the servant as his lord. If they have called the master of the house Beelzebub, how much more shall they call them of his household?" (Matt. 10:25). I believe if we were more like Christ we should be much more loved by His friends and much more hated by His enemies. I do not believe the world would be half so lenient to the Church nowadays if it were not that the Church has grown complacent to the world. When any of us speak up boldly, selfish motives are imputed to us, our language is turned upside down, and we are abhorred of men. We get smooth things, because I am afraid we are too much like the prophets who prophesied peace, peace, where there was no peace. Let us be true to our Master, stand out and come out and be like Him, and we must expect the same treatment that He had.

Christ Will Appear

The text speaks of it as a fact to be taken for granted. "When Christ, who is our life, shall appear." It is not a matter of question in the Church whether Christ will appear or not. Has not Christ appeared once? Yes, after a certain sort. I remember reading a quaint expression of some old divine that the book of Revelation might quite as well be called an Obvelation, for it was rather a hiding than a revealing of things to come. So when Jesus came, it was hardly a revealing; it was a hiding of our Lord. It is true that He was "manifest in the flesh" (1 Tim. 3:16), but it is equally true that the flesh shrouded and concealed His glory. The first manifestation was very partial; it was Christ seen through a glass, Christ in the mist of grief and the cloud of humiliation. Christ is yet to appear in the strong sense of the word *appearing*; He is to come out and shine forth. He is to leave the robes of scorn and shame behind and to come in the glory of the Father and all His holy angels with Him. This is the constant teaching of the Word of God and the constant hope of the Church, that *Christ will appear*. A thousand questions at once suggest themselves: How will Christ appear? When? Where? and so on. What God answers we may inquire, but some of our questions are mere impertinence.

How will Christ appear? I believe Christ will appear in person. Whenever I think of the second coming, I never can tolerate the idea of a spiritual coming. That always seems to me to be the most transparent folly that can possibly be put together, because Christ cannot come spiritually to where He already always is: "Lo, I am with you alway, even unto the end of the world" (Matt. 28:20). I believe in a personal reign and coming of our Lord Jesus Christ, and there is an abundance of Scriptures that support this fact.

But how will He come? He will doubtless come with great splendor; the angels of God shall be His attendants. We gather from Scripture that He will come to reign in the midst of His people, that the house of Israel will acknowledge Him as King, yea, that all nations shall bow down before Him, and kings shall pay Him homage. None shall be able to stand against Him. "Behold, he cometh with clouds; and every eye shall see him, and they also which pierced him: and all kindreds of the earth shall wail because of him" (Rev. 1:7). He will come to discern between the righteous and the wicked, to separate the goats from the sheep. He will come graciously to adjudge His people their reward according to their works. He will give to those who have been faithful over a few things to be rulers over many things, and those who have been faithful over many things shall be rulers over many cities. He will come to discern between the works of His people; such as are only wood, hay, and stubble will be consumed; such as are gold, silver, and precious stones will stand the fire. He will come to condemn the wicked to eternal punishment and to take His people up to their everlasting mansions in the skies. We look for such a coming, and without entering into minute details, drawing charts, and painting pictures, we are content to believe that He is coming in His glory to show Himself to be what He ever was—King of kings and Lord of lords, God over all, blessed forever, to be adored and worshiped, and no more to be despised and rejected of men.

When will He come? That is a question that unbelief asks with a start. Faith replies, "It is not for you to know the times or the seasons, which the Father hath put in his own power" (Acts 1:7). Some simpleton says, "But we may know the week, month, or year." Do not trifle with God's Word and make a fool of yourself, because you must know that the expression means that you do not know anything about the time at all, and you never will know. Christ will come in a time when we do not look for Him, just perhaps when the world and the Church are most asleep. When the wise and the foolish virgins have alike fallen into a deep slumber, when the stewards shall begin to beat their fellow servants and to drink and to be drunken, He will come like a thief, and the house shall be suddenly broken up. But come He will, and that is enough for you and for me to know. And when He comes, we shall appear, for as *He* shall appear, *we* shall also appear with Him in glory.

When Christ Appears, We Also Shall Appear

Do you ever feel like those lions in the zoo, restlessly pacing before the bars of their cage and seeming to feel that they were never meant to be confined within those narrow limits? Sometimes they are for thrusting their heads through the bars and then for dashing back and tearing the back of their dungeon or for ripping up the surface beneath them as if they yearned for liberty. Do you ever feel like that? Does your soul ever want to get free from her cage? Here is an iron bar of sin, of doubt, and there is another iron bar of mistrust and weakness. Oh, if you could tear them away, could get rid of them all, you would do something for Christ—you would be like Christ! Oh, if you could but by some means or other burst the bands of this captivity! But you cannot, and therefore you feel uneasy. You may have seen an eagle with a chain upon its foot, standing on a rock—poor unhappy thing! It flaps its wings—looks up to the sun—wants to fly right straight ahead at it and stare the sun out of countenance—looks to the blue sky and seems as if it could sniff the blue beyond the dusky clouds, and wants to be away, and so it tries its wings and dreams of mounting—but that *chain*, that *cruel chain*, remorselessly holds it down.

Has it not often been so with you? You feel, "I am not meant to be what I am, I am sure I am not. I have a something in me that is adapted for something better and higher, and I want to mount and soar, but that chain—that dragging chain of the body of sin and death will keep me down." Now it is to such as you that this text comes and says, "Yes, your present state is not your soul's true condition. You have a hidden life in you; that life of yours pants to get out of the bonds and fetters that control it, and it shall be delivered soon, for Christ is coming, and when Christ shall appear, you shall appear—the same appearance that belongs to Him belongs to you. He shall come, and then your day of true happiness and joy and peace and everything that you are panting for and longing for shall certainly come too."

I wonder whether the little oak inside the acorn—for there is a whole oak there, and there are all the roots and all the boughs and everything inside that acorn—I wonder whether that little oak inside the acorn ever has any premonition of the summer weather that will float over it a hundred years later and of the mists that will hang in autumn on its withered leaves and of the hundreds of acorns that it will cast every autumn upon the earth, when it shall become in the forest a great tree. You and I are like that acorn; inside of each of us are the seeds of great things. There is the tree that we are to be—I mean there is the spiritual thing we are to be, both in body and soul even now within us. And sometimes here below, in happy moments, we get some inklings of what we are to be; and then how we want to burst the shell, to get out of the acorn and to be the oak!

I do not know what I am to become, but I feel that there is a heart within me too big for these ribs to hold. I have an immortal spark that cannot have been intended to burn on this poor earth and then to go out; it must have been meant to burn on heaven's altar. Wait a bit, and when Christ comes you will know what you are. We are in the metamorphic state now, and those who are the liveliest caterpillars among us grow more and more uneasy in that changing state. Others are so frozen up in it that they forget the hereafter and appear content to remain a caterpillar forever. But some of us feel that we would sooner not be than be what we now are forever. We feel as if we must burst our bonds, and when that time of bursting shall come, when the caterpillar shall get its painted wings and mount to the land of flowers, then shall we be satisfied. The text tells us—"When Christ, who is our life, shall *appear*"—when He comes out in all His glory—"we also shall appear with him in glory." If you would like these gracious promises drawn out into detail with regard to the body, you may listen to just such words as these: "It is sown a natural body: it is raised a spiritual body.... The first man is of the earth, earthy: the second man is the Lord from heaven. As is the earthy, such are they also that are earthy: and as is the heavenly, such are they also that are heavenly" (1 Cor. 15:44, 47–48). Whatever Christ's body is in heaven, our body is to be like it: whatever its glory and strength and power, our corruptible body is to be fashioned like unto His glorious body. As for our soul, whatever of absolute perfection—whatever of immortal joy Christ possesses, we are to possess that; and as for honor—whatever of esteem and love Christ may have from intelligent beings, we are to share in the same; and as for position before God—whatever Christ has—we are to stand where He stands.

Are His enemies put to confusion? So are ours. Do all worlds discern His glory? They shall discern ours, too. Is all dishonor wiped away from Him? So shall it be from us. Do they forget forever the shame and spitting, the cross and the nails? So shall they in our case. Is it forever "Glory! and honor! and power! and dominion! and bliss without end?" So shall it be in our case. Let us comfort one another, therefore, with these words and look up out of our metamorphosis to that happier and better day when we shall be like Him, for we shall see Him as He is.

Christ will be admired and adored because of this grand result. O mighty Master, with what amazing moral alchemy did you work to turn that morose dispositioned man into a mass of love! How did you work to lift that selfish money lover up from his hoarded gains to make him find his gain in You? How did You overcome that proud spirit, that fickle spirit, that lazy spirit, that lustful spirit—how did You devise to take all these away? How did You exterminate the very roots of sin, and every little runner of sin, out of Your redeemed so that not a tiny fiber can be found? "In that time, saith the Lord, the iniquity of Israel shall be sought for, and there shall be none; and the sins of Judah, and they shall not be found" (Jer. 50:20). Neither the guilt of sin nor the propensity to sin—both shall be gone, and Christ shall have done it, and He will be "glorified in his saints, and admired in all them that believe."

Chapter Nine

Jesus Admired in Those Who Believe

When he shall come to be glorified in his saints, and to be admired in all them that believe (because our testimony among you was believed) in that day—2 Thessalonians 1:10.

WHAT A DIFFERENCE between the first and second comings of our Lord! When He shall come a second time, it will be to be glorified and admired; when He came the first time, it was to be despised and rejected of men. He comes a second time to reign with unexampled splendor, but the first time He came to die in circumstances of shame and sorrow. Lift up your eyes, you children of light, and anticipate the change that will be as great for you as for your Lord, for now you are hidden even as He was hidden and misunderstood even as He was misunderstood when He walked among the sons of men. "We know that, when he shall appear, we shall be like him; for we shall see him as he is" (1 John 3:2). His manifestation will be our manifestation, and in the day in which He is revealed in glory, then shall His saints be glorified with Him.

Observe that our Lord is spoken of as coming in His glory and as at the same time taking vengeance in flaming fire on those who do not know God and do not obey the gospel (2 Thess. 1:8). This is a note of great terror to all who are ignorant of God and wickedly unbelieving concerning His Christ. Let them take heed, for the Lord will gain glory by the overthrow of His enemies, and those who would not bow before Him cheerfully shall be compelled to bow before Him abjectly. They shall crouch at His feet, and at the glance of His eyes they shall utterly wither away; as it is written, they "shall be punished with everlasting destruction from the presence of the Lord, and from the glory of his power" (2 Thess. 1:9).

But this is not the main reason for which Christ will come, nor is this the matter in which He finds His chief glory. To destroy the wicked is a matter of necessity in which His spirit takes no delight, for He does this, according to the text, not so much when He comes to do it as when He shall come with another object, namely, "to be glorified in his saints, and to be admired in all them that believe."

The crowning honor of Christ will be seen in His people, and this is the design with which He will return to this earth in the latter days, that He may be glorious in His saints and exceedingly magnified in them. Even now His saints glorify Him. When they walk in holiness, they reflect His light; their holy deeds are beams from Him who is the Sun of righteousness. When they believe in Him, they also glorify Him, for there is no grace that pays lowlier homage at the throne of Jesus than the grace of faith whereby we trust Him and so confess Him to be our All in all. We do glorify our gracious Lord, but we must all confess that we do not do this as we could desire, for, alas, too often we dishonor Him and grieve His Holy Spirit. By our lack of zeal and by our many sins we are guilty of discrediting His gospel and dishonoring His name. Happy, happy, happy day when this shall no more be possible, when we shall be rid of the inward corruption that now works itself into outward sin, and shall never dishonor Christ again, but shall shine with a clear, pure radiance, like the moon on the Passover night when it looks the sun full in the face and then shines upon the earth at her best.

The Special Glorification

The first point to note is *the time*. The text says, "When he shall come to be glorified in his saints." The full glorification of Christ in His saints will be when He shall come a second time, according to the sure word of prophecy. He is glorified in them now, for He says, "All mine are thine, and thine are mine; and I am glorified in them" (John 17:10), but as yet that glory is perceptible to Jesus rather than to the outer world. The lamps are being trimmed, they will shine before long. These are the days of preparation before that Sabbath that is in an infinite sense a high day. As it was said of Esther, that for so many months she prepared herself with myrrh and sweet odors before she entered the king's palace to be espoused of him, even so are we now being purified and made ready for that august day when the perfected Church shall be presented to Christ as a bride to her husband. John says of her that she shall be "prepared as a bride adorned for her husband" (Rev. 21:2). This is our night, when we must watch; but behold, the morning comes, a morning without clouds, and then shall we walk in a sevenfold light because our Well-beloved has come. His second advent will be His revelation: He was under a cloud here, and men perceived Him not, save only a few who beheld His glory; but when He comes a second time, all veils will be removed, and every eye shall see the glory of His countenance. For this He waits, and His Church waits with Him.

Note also *in whom* this glorification of Christ is to be found. The text says that He will be glorified not "*by* his saints" but "*in* his saints." There is more than a shade of difference between the two terms. We endeavor to glorify Him now by our actions, but then He will be glorified in our own persons and character and condition. He is glorified *by* what we do, but He is at the last to be glorified *in* what we are. Who are these in whom Jesus is to be glorified and admired? They are spoken of under two descriptions: "in his saints" and "in all them that believe."

In "his saints" first. All those in whom Christ will be glorified are described as holy ones or saints: men and women who have been sanctified and made pure, whose gracious lives show that they have been under the teaching of the Holy Spirit, whose obedient actions prove that they are disciples of a Holy Master, even of Him "who is holy, harmless, undefiled, separate from sinners, and made higher than the heavens" (Heb. 7:26). But inasmuch as these saints are also said to be believers, I gather that the holiness that will honor Christ at last is a holiness based on faith in Him, a holiness of which this was the root—that they first trusted in Christ, and then, being saved, they loved their Lord and obeyed Him. Their faith worked by love and purified their souls and so cleansed their lives. It is an inner as well as an outer purity, arising out of the living and operative principle of faith. If anyone thinks that he can attain to holiness apart from faith in Christ, he is as much mistaken as he who hopes to reap a harvest without casting seed into the ground. Faith is the bulb, and saintliness is the delightfully fragrant flower that comes of it when planted in the soil of a renewed heart. Beware, I pray you, of any pretense to a holiness arising out of yourself and maintained by the energy of your own unaided will; it is like expecting to gather grapes of thorns or figs of thistles.

I would call your attention once again to the second description: "all them that believe." This is enlarged by the hint that they are believers in a certain testimony, according to the parenthetical clause—"because our testimony among you was believed." Now, the testimony of the apostles was concerning Christ. They saw Him in His physical body, and they bore witness that "God was manifest in the flesh" (1 Tim. 3:16); they saw His holy life, and they bore witness to it; they saw His death of grief, and they witnessed that "God was in Christ, reconciling the world unto himself" (2 Cor. 5:19); they saw Him risen from the dead, and they said, "This Jesus hath God raised up, whereof we all are witnesses" (Acts 2:32); they saw Him rise into heaven, and they bore witness that God had taken Him up to His right hand. Now, all who believe this witness are saved. "If thou shalt confess with thy mouth the Lord Jesus, and shalt believe in thine heart that God hath raised him from the dead, thou shalt be saved" (Rom. 10:9). All who with a simple faith come and cast themselves upon the fact of the incarnate God, living and dying for men and ever sitting at the right hand of God to make intercession for them—these are the people in whom Christ will be glorified and admired at the last great day. But inasmuch as they are first said to be saints, be it never forgotten that this faith must be a living faith, a faith that produces a hatred of sin, a faith that renews the character and shapes the life after the noble model of Christ, thus turning sinners into saints.

But now a question arises: *by whom* will Christ be thus glorified and admired? He shines in His people, but who will see the glory? I answer first that His people will see it. Every saint will glorify Christ in himself and admire Christ in himself. He will say, "What a wonder that such a poor creature as I am should be thus perfected! How glorious is my Lord, who has wrought this miracle upon me!" This I know, that when I personally enter heaven, I shall forever admire and adore the everlasting love that brought me there. Yes, we will all glorify and admire our Savior for what He has accomplished in us by His infinite grace.

The saints will also admire Christ in one another. As I shall see you and you shall see your brothers and sisters in Christ all perfect, you will be filled with wonderment and gratitude and delight. You will be free from all envy there, and therefore you will rejoice in all the beauty of your fellow saints. Their heaven will be a heaven to you, and what a multitude of heavens you will have as you will joy in the joy of all the redeemed! We shall as much admire the Lord's handiwork in others as in ourselves and shall each one praise Him for saving all the rest.

But that will not be all. Besides the redeemed and ransomed of Christ, there will be on that great day of His coming all the holy angels to stand by and look on and wonder. They marveled much when first He stooped from heaven to earth, and they desired to look into those things that were then a mystery to them. But when they shall see their beloved Prince come back with ten thousand times ten thousand of the ransomed at His feet, all of them made perfect by having washed their robes and made them white in His blood, how the principalities and powers will admire Him in every one of His redeemed!

We do not know what other races of innocent creatures there may be, but I think it is no stretch of the imagination to believe that as this world is only one speck in the creation of God, there may be millions of other races in the countless worlds around us, and all these may be invited to behold the wonders of redeeming love as manifested in the saints in the day of the Lord. I seem to see these unfallen intelligences encompassing the saints as a cloud of witnesses and in rapt vision beholding in them the love and grace of the redeeming Lord. What songs! What shouts shall rise from all these to the praise of the ever blessed God! What an orchestra of praise will the universe become! From star to star the holy hymn shall roll till all space shall ring out the hosannas of wondering spirits.

Then shall Satan and his defeated legions and the lost spirits of ungodly men bite their lips with envy and rage and tremble at the majesty of Jesus in that day. By their confessed defeat and manifest despair they shall glorify Him in His people, in whom they have been utterly overthrown. They shall see that there is not one lost whom He redeemed by blood, not one snatched away of all the sheep His Father gave Him, not one warrior enlisted beneath His banner fallen in the day of battle, but all more than conquerors through Him who loved them. What despair shall seize upon diabolic spirits as they discover their entire defeat! Defeated in men who were once their slaves! Jesus, triumphant by taking the lambs from the lion's jaws and rescuing His feeble sheep from their power, will utterly put them to shame in His redeemed.

You see then that there are enough spectators to magnify Christ in His saints, and so let us inquire *in what degree* will the Lord Jesus be glorified? Our answer is, it will be to the very highest degree. He shall come to be glorified in His saints to the utmost, for this is clear from the words, "to be admired." When our translation was made, the word *admired* had a stronger flavor of wonder than it has to us now. We often speak of admiring a thing in the softer sense of loving it, but the real meaning of the English word and of the Greek also is *wonder*: our Lord will be wondered at in all who believe. Those who look upon the saints will feel a sudden wonderment of sacred delight; they will be startled with the surprising glory of the Lord's work in them. "We thought He would do great things, but this! This surpasses our dreams!" Every saint will be a wonder to himself. "I thought my bliss would be great, but nothing like this!" All His brethren will be a wonder to the perfected believer, who will say, "I thought the saints would be perfect, but I never imagined such a transfiguration of excessive glory would be put upon each of them. I could not have imagined my Lord to be so good and gracious." The angels in heaven will say that they never anticipated such deeds of grace: they did know that He had undertaken a great work, but they did not know that He would do so much for His people and in His people. The men who once despised the saints, who called them two-faced hypocrites and trampled on them and perhaps slew them, the kings and princes of the earth who sold the righteous for a pair of shoes, what will they say when they see the least of the Savior's followers become a prince of more illustrious rank than the great ones of the earth, and Christ shining out in every one of these favored beings?

My next point leads us into the very heart of the subject: *in what respects* will Christ be glorified and wondered at? I cannot expect to tell you one tenth of it. I am going to give you but a little sample of what this must mean; exhaustive exposition would be quite impossible to me. I think with regard to His saints that Jesus will be glorified and wondered at on account of their number—"a great multitude, which no man could number" (Rev. 7:9). John was a great mathematician, and he managed to count up to one hundred and forty-four thousand of all the tribes of the children of Israel, but that was only a representative number for the Jewish church. For the Church of God, comprehending the Gentile nations, John gave up all idea of counting and confessed that it was beyond computing. When he heard them sing, he says, "I heard a voice from heaven, as the voice of many waters, and as the voice of a great thunder" (Rev. 14:2). There were so many of them that their song was like the Mediterranean Sea lashed to fury by a tempest, nay, not one great sea in uproar but ocean upon ocean, the Atlantic and the Pacific piled upon each other, and the Arctic upon these, and other oceans upon these, layers of oceans, all thundering out their mightiest roar: and such will be the song of the redeemed, for the crowds that swell the matchless hymn will be beyond all reckoning.

Behold, you who laughed at His kingdom, and see how the little one has become a thousand! Now look, you foes of Christ, and see how the handful of seed now flourishes like the grass of the earth. Who can count the drops of the dew or the sands on the seashore? When they have counted these, they shall not have guessed at the multitude of the redeemed whom Christ shall bring to glory. And all this harvest from one grain of wheat, which except it had fallen into the ground and died would have remained alone! Who said the word, "If it die, it bringeth forth much fruit" (John 12:24)? Is not the prophecy fulfilled? O beloved, what a harvest from the lone Man of Nazareth!

But there is quality as well as quantity. Jesus is admired in His saints because every one of them is living proof of His power to save from evil. My eye can hardly bear, even though it is only in my imagination at this moment, to gaze upon the glittering ranks of the white-robed ones, where each one outshines the sun, and they are all as if a sevenfold midday had clothed them. Yet all these, as I look at them, tell me, "We have washed our robes, for they were once defiled. We have made them white, but this whiteness is caused by the blood of the Lamb." These were children of wrath even as others; these were dead in trespasses and sins; all these like sheep had gone astray and turned every one to his own way. But look at them and see how He has saved them, washed them, cleansed them, perfected them! His power and grace are seen in all of them. If your eye will pause here and there, you will discover some who were supremely stubborn, whose neck was as iron, and yet He conquered them by love. Some were willfully ignorant, but

He opened their blind eyes. Some were grossly infected with the leprosy of lust, but He healed them. Some were under Satan's most terrible power, but He cast the devil out of them. Oh, how He will be glorified in special cases! In the drunkard made into a saint, in the blasphemer turned into a loving disciple, in the persecutor who breathed out threatenings taught to sing everlastingly a hymn of praise! Jesus will be exceedingly glorified in such.

Perhaps the chief point in which Christ will be glorified will be the absolute perfection of all the saints. They shall then be "not having spot, or wrinkle, or any such thing" (Eph. 5:27). We have not experienced what perfection is, and therefore we can hardly conceive it; our thoughts themselves are too sinful for us to get a full idea of what absolute perfection must be; but we shall have no sin left in us, "for they are without fault before the throne of God" (Rev. 14:5), and we shall have no remaining propensity to sin. There shall be no bias in the will toward that which is evil, but it shall be fixed forever upon that which is good. The affections will never be licentious again; they will be chaste for Christ. The understanding will never make mistakes. You shall never put bitter for sweet, nor sweet for bitter; you shall be "perfect, even as your Father which is in heaven is perfect" (Matt. 5:48); and truly, He who works this in us will be a wonder.

Christ will be admired and adored because of this grand result. O mighty Master, with what amazing moral alchemy did you work to turn that morose dispositioned man into a mass of love! How did you work to lift that selfish money lover up from his hoarded gains to make him find his gain in You? How did You overcome that proud spirit, that fickle spirit, that lazy spirit, that lustful spirit—how did You devise to take all these away? How did You exterminate the very roots of sin, and every little runner of sin, out of Your redeemed so that not a tiny fiber can be found? "In that time, saith the LORD, the iniquity of Israel shall be sought for, and there shall be none; and the sins of Judah, and they shall not be found" (Jer. 50:20). Neither the guilt of sin nor the propensity to sin—both shall be gone, and Christ shall have done it, and He will be "glorified in his saints, and admired in all them that believe."

This is only the beginning, however. There will be seen in every saint, in that last wondrous day, the wisdom and power and love of Christ in having brought them through all the trials of the way. He kept their faith alive when it would have died out; He sustained them under trials when they would have fainted; He held them fast in their integrity when temptation solicited them and they had almost slipped with their feet. Ay, He sustained some of them in prison and on the rack and at the stake and held them faithful still! One might hardly wish to be a martyr, but I reckon that the martyrs will be the admiration of us all, or rather Christ will be admired in them. However they could bear such pain as some of them did endure for Christ's sake, none of us can guess, except that we know that Christ was in them suffering in His members. Eternally will Jesus be wondered at in them as all intelligent spirits shall see how He upheld them so that neither tribulation nor distress nor nakedness nor famine nor sword could separate them from His love.

Remember that we shall see in that day how the blessed Christ, as "head over all things to the church" (Eph. 1:22), has ruled every providence to the sanctification of His people—how the dark days eventually brought the showers that made the plants of the Lord to grow, how the fierce sun that threatened to scorch them to the root filled them with warmth of love divine and ripened their choice fruit. What a tale the saints will have to tell of how that which threatened to put out the fire of grace made it burn more mightily, how the stone that threatened to kill their faith was turned into bread for them, how the rod and staff of the Good Shepherd was ever with them to bring them safely home.

I cannot stop over this, but I must beg you to notice that as a king is glorious in his regalia, so will Christ put on His saints as His personal splendor in that day when He shall make up His jewels. It is with Christ as it was with that noble Roman matron who, when she called at her friends' houses and saw their trinkets, asked them to come next day to her house and she would exhibit her jewels. They expected to see ruby and pearl and diamond, but she called in her two boys and said, "These are my jewels." Even so will Jesus, instead of emerald and amethyst and onyx and topaz, exhibit His saints. "These are my choice treasures," says He, "in whom I will be glorified." Solomon surely was never more full of glory than when he had finished the temple, when all the tribes came together to see the noble structure and confessed it to be "beautiful for situation, the joy of the whole earth" (Ps. 48:2). But what will be the glory of Christ when all the living stones shall be put into their places and His Church shall have her windows of agate and her gates of carbuncle and all her borders of precious stones. Then, indeed, will He be glorified, when the twelve foundations of His new Jerusalem shall be courses of stones most precious, the like of which was never seen.

Inasmuch as my text lays special emphasis upon *believing*, I invite you to consider how as believers as well as saints the saved ones will glorify their Lord.

First, it will be wonderful that there should be so many brought to faith in Christ: men with no God and men with many gods, men steeped in ignorance and men puffed up with carnal wisdom, great men and poor men, all brought to believe in the one Redeemer and praise Him for His great salvation. Will He not be glorified in their common faith? It will magnify Him that they will all be saved by faith and not by their own merits.

I want you to reflect that Jesus will be glorified in the risen bodies of all His saints. Now, in heaven, they are pure spirits, but when He shall come, they shall be clothed again. Poor body, you must sleep awhile, but what you shall be at your awaking does not yet appear. You are now the shriveled seed, but there is a flower to come of you that shall be lovely beyond all thought. Though sown in weakness, this body shall be raised in power; though sown in corruption, it shall be raised in incorruption (1 Cor. 15:42–43). Weakness, weariness, pain, and death will be banished forever; infirmity and deformity will be all unknown. The Lord will raise up our bodies to be like His glorious body. Oh, what a prospect lies before us! Let us remember that His blessed resurrection will come to us because He rose, for there must be a resurrection to the members because the Head has risen. Oh, the charm of being a risen man perfect in body, soul, and spirit! All that charm will be due to Christ, and therefore He will be admired in us.

Then let us think of the absolute perfection of the Church as to numbers: all who have believed in Him will be with Him in glory. The text says, He will be "admired in *all* them that believe." Now, if some of those who believe perished, He would not be admired in them, but they will all be there, the little ones as well as the great ones. You will be there, even when those of you who say, "Lord, I believe," are obliged to add, "help thou mine unbelief" (Mark 9:24). He shall be admired in all believers without a single exception, and there shall probably be more wonder at the going to heaven of the weak believers than of the stronger ones.

John Bunyan's Mr. Greatheart, when he comes to heaven, will owe his victories to his Master and lay his laurels at His feet; but fainting Feeble-mind and limping Ready-to-halt with his crutches and trembling Little-faith, when they enter into rest, will make heaven ring with notes of even greater admiration that such poor creatures of the earth should win the day by mighty grace. Suppose that one of them should be missing at last! Stop the harps! Silence the songs! No beginning to be merry while one child is shut out! It is the glory of Jesus that as the Shepherd He has lost none of His flock, as the Captain of salvation He has brought many sons to glory and has lost none, and hence He is admired, not in some who believe, nor yet in all but one, but He is "admired in *all* them that believe."

Another point of admiration will be the eternal safety of all His believing people. There they are safe from fear of harm. You dogs of hell howled at their heels and hoped to devour them, but they have escaped from you! What must it be to be lifted above gunshot of the enemy, where no more watch shall need to be kept, for even the roar of the satanic artillery cannot be heard? O glorious Christ, to bring them all to such a state of safety, You are indeed to be wondered at forever.

Moreover, all the saints will be so honored, so happy, and so like their Lord that they and everything about them will be themes for never-ending admiration. Perhaps you have been in a room that was hung round with mirrors, and when you stood in the middle you were reflected from every point: you were seen here and seen there and there again and there again, and so every part of you was reflected. In heaven, Jesus is the center, and all His saints like mirrors reflect His glory. Is He human? So are they! Is He the Son of God? So are they sons of God! Is He perfect? So are they! Is He exalted? So are they! Is He a prophet? So are they, making known to the principalities and powers the manifold wisdom of God. Is He a priest? So are they! Is He a King? So are they, for He has made us priests and kings to God, and we shall reign forever and ever. Look anywhere along the ranks of the redeemed, and this one thing shall be seen: the glory of Christ Jesus, even to surprise and wonder.

Practical Suggestions

First, the text suggests that the principal subject for self-examination with us all should be—Am I a saint? Am I holy? Am I a believer in Christ? Yes or no, for on that yes or no must hang your glorification of Christ or your banishment from His presence.

The next thing is—observe the small value of human opinion. When Christ was here, the world reckoned Him to be a nobody, and while His people are here, they must expect to be judged in the same way. What do unbelievers know about it? How soon will their judgment be reversed! When our Lord shall appear, even those who sneered will be compelled to admire. When they shall see the glory of Christ in every one of His people, awestricken, they will have nothing to say against us; nay, not even the false tongue of malicious slander shall dare to hiss out a serpent word in that day. Never mind them, then; put up with the reproach that shall so soon be silenced.

The next suggestion is a great encouragement to inquirers who are seeking Christ, for I put it to you, if Jesus is to be glorified in saved sinners, would He not be glorified indeed if He saved you? If He were ever to save such a rebel as you have been, would it not be the astonishment of eternity? What if my Master were to make a saint of you! Bad raw material! Yet suppose He transformed you into a precious jewel and made you to be as holy as God is holy, what would you say of Him? "Say of Him," you say. "I would praise Him world without end." Yes, and you shall do so if you will come and trust Him. Put your trust in Him.

Our text gives an exhortation to believers also. Will Jesus Christ be honored and glorified in all the saints? Then let us think well of them all and love them all. Some dear children of God have unattractive bodies, or they are blind or deformed or maimed; and many of them are poor, and it may be the church knows most of them as coming for financial help. Moreover, they have little knowledge, little power to please, and they are uncouth in manners and belong to what are called the lowest ranks of society. Do not, therefore, despise them, for one day our Lord will be glorified in them. How He will be admired in the poor bedridden woman when she rises from the poorhouse to sing hallelujah to God and the Lamb among the brightest of the shining ones. Why, I think the pain, the poverty, the weakness, and the sorrow of saints below will greatly glorify the Captain of their salvation as they tell how grace helped them to bear their burdens and to rejoice under their afflictions.

Finally, this text ought to encourage all of you who love Jesus to go on talking about Him to others and bearing your testimony for His name. You see how the apostle Paul has inserted a few words by way of parentheses. Draw the words out of the brackets and take them home: "because our testimony among you was believed." Do you see the crowds of former idolatrous heathen and the hosts of saved ones before the throne of God? What is the medium that linked the two characters? By what visible means did the sinners become saints? Do you see that insignificant-looking man with weak eyes? That man whose bodily presence is weak and whose speech is contemptible? Do you not see that he has been making and mending tents, for he is only a tentmaker. Now, those bright spirits that shine like suns, flashing forth Christ's glory, were made thus bright through the messages and prayers of that tentmaker. The Thessalonians were heathens plunged in sin, and this poor tentmaker came in among them and told them of Jesus Christ and His gospel, his testimony was believed, that belief changed the lives of his hearers and made them holy, and they being renewed came at length to be perfectly holy, and there they are, and Jesus Christ is glorified in them. Hallelujah!

Will it not be a delightful thing throughout eternity to contemplate that you went into your Sunday-school class, and though were afraid you could not say much, you talked about Jesus Christ with a tear in your eye, and you brought a dear girl to believe in His saving name through your testimony. In years to come, that girl will be among those who shine out to the glory of Christ forever. Or you will tell some of those poor, despised tramps or homeless or one of the fallen women the story of your Lord's love and blood, and the poor broken heart will catch at the gracious word and come to Jesus, and then a heavenly character will begin and another jewel secured for the Redeemer's diadem. I think you will admire His crown all the more because, as you see certain stones sparkling in it, you will say, "Blessed be His name forever, for He helped me to dive into the sea and find that pearl for Him, and now it adorns His sacred brow."

If you stand at the seaside, you have noticed that at certain hours of the day there is a long expanse of mud or of dry sand, and it may not seem to one who sees it for the first time as though the sea had ever rolled over it or that it ever will. Ah, but "it doth not yet appear" what it will be. It is ebb tide now, but wait till the flood comes, and then you will see the whole of that black mire or that yellow sand glistening in the sunshine. So the flood of glory is rising for the believer in Christ; can you not see the breakers in the distance, the white crests of the incoming waves? God's great sea of eternity draws nearer and nearer; can you not hear the booming of that mighty flood? Soon shall your ransomed spirit float and bathe in that sea of glory, where not a single wave shall cause you a moment's grief or pain. This is not the time in which you are to be fully revealed. You are, today, like that ugly, shriveled seed; there is no beauty in it that you should desire it. But wait a little while, and when the sweetly perfumed flower shall shed its fragrance on the air and make the gazer pause to admire the matchless colors with which God has been pleased to paint it, then shall its full glory be known and seen. At present, you are in your seed stage, and your sowing time is coming. Tremble not that it is so. There will be a time for your poor flesh to sleep in the silent grave, but at the voice of the archangel and the blast of the trumpet of the resurrection, you shall arise. Just as the flower rises in spring, the dead body that was put into the tomb shall rise incorruptible in the image of the Savior.

Chapter Ten

The Christian's Manifestation

Beloved, now are we the sons of God, and it doth not yet appear what we shall be: but we know that, when he shall appear, we shall be like him; for we shall see him as he is—1 John 3:2.

THE TEXT MENTIONS "now," and then passes on to the future and speaks of "yet." It does, however, speak of "now," for after all, despite our trials, there is much to make us happy in our present condition. "Beloved, *now* are we the sons of God." Our manifold temptations and weaknesses cannot make us lose the blessings that come to us through our adoption into the family of God. "Happy art thou, O Israel: who is like unto thee, O people saved by the LORD" (Deut. 33:29). Today, even today, we are the blessed of the Lord, and we find in godliness tremendous blessings.

But if this were all our life, it would have been better for us not to have lived. Young says, "Were there no death, e'en fools might wish to die," and wise men would do so without question. This is a life of distractions, cares, anxieties, disappointments, and what is worse, it is a life of sins and sorrows and bitter repentances for wrongdoing. This life is to us a transitory life; we are here today and gone tomorrow. Sometimes the heat consumes us, and at other times the cold bites us. We are like men at sea: we have not yet cast our anchor nor furled our sails nor reached the port where we are bound, and the sea on which we are sailing is rough and tempest-tossed and beset with rocks and shoals and quicksands. Our soul is often in great distress and longs for the desired haven where "the wicked cease from troubling; and there the weary be at rest" (Job 3:17). Ours is a soldier's life; we have to be constantly fighting or else continually upon our guard. Think not, you who have just taken up the sword, that you have won the victory, for the good soldiers of Jesus Christ must fight from morning till evening, from youth's happy morning till the evening of gray old age.

I would not paint life in sadder colors than it needs, but I dare not shut my eyes to the fact that this is a sad world and that our path is one of sorrow, for "we must through much tribulation enter into the kingdom of God" (Acts 14:22). It is to that other and better land that I would lift your thoughts. We shall borrow the wings of our text and, like the eagle, soar toward heaven.

"It Doth Not Yet Appear What We Shall Be"

What we are to be we can scarcely guess. Indeed, we cannot guess at all merely by the use of our natural senses. "Eye hath not seen, nor ear heard, neither have entered into the heart of man, the things which God hath prepared for them that love him. But God hath revealed them unto us by his Spirit" (1 Cor. 2:9–10)—but only to our spirit. Flesh and blood cannot inherit the kingdom of God or even guess what that kingdom is like. This is not the place where the Christian is to be seen. This is the place of his veiling; heaven is the place of his manifestation. Our portion is on the other side of the river; our days of feasting are not yet.

Some of the reasons why "it doth not yet appear what we shall be" may be as follows. First, *our Master was, to a great extent, concealed and hidden, and we must expect to be as He was.* Is it not written in this very epistle, "As he is, so are we in this world" (1 John 4:17)? Jesus said to His followers when He was here upon earth, "The disciple is not above his master, nor the servant above his lord. It is enough for the disciple that he be as his master, and the servant as his lord" (Matt. 10:24–25). See that man, the carpenter's son, the heir of poverty, the companion of the humblest masses of mankind. Can you see in Him God over all, blessed forever? If you can, you are not looking with the eyes of your flesh, I am sure, for in that manner, you cannot detect the glory of the Lord Jesus Christ beneath so humble a garb. The veil that the Savior cast about

Himself was not so thick but that some rays of His glory burst through when He trod the waves and rebuked the winds and raised the dead, but still, it was sufficiently dense, for He cried, "The foxes have holes, and the birds of the air have nests; but the Son of man hath not where to lay his head" (Matt. 8:20).

You will see that Christ was concealed as you recollect that although, as Dr. Watts says, "All riches are His native right," yet when He had to pay the temple tax, He had to work a miracle so that Peter might be able to catch the fish that had the exact amount required in its mouth. Jesus was so poor that He had to live upon the charity of His followers. Would you have believed that *He* was the Lord of all creation if you had seen Him up on that lonely mountainside without a bed to rest upon or sitting wearily upon Jacob's well at Sychar and asking a sinful woman to give Him a little water to drink? The Savior was, indeed, masked and hidden so that the common eye could not detect His glory. Only such eagle-eyed men as John were able to say, "(And we beheld his glory, the glory as of the only begotten of the Father,) full of grace and truth" (John 1:14). Our Lord's wisdom and grace and power and all His other illustrious attributes were concealed beneath the veil of our inferior clay. So fully did He veil His glory that some even ventured so far as to call Him Beelzebub and to say that He was a gluttonous man and a wine bibber!

It should come as no surprise, then, if unbelievers do not know you and only speak of you to slander you. Do you wonder if your integrity is questioned and your most manifest virtue is misrepresented and if the grace that really is within you is criticized and despised? How should the world know you when the Savior Himself was not discovered? As the bright gleams of His divine glory were almost wholly concealed, surely the weaker gleams of your earthly and human glory must be altogether hidden.

I think I may also remark that we *are not yet fully prepared to let it appear what we shall be.* One may wonder at times why the son in a wealthy house is treated as if he were a servant, and even worse than if he were a servant, for he may come under stern discipline. Why does not his father give him the honor and dignity that belong to his sonship? Simply because he is at present only a child, and he must be treated as a child for a time so that he may be prepared to adorn his sonship. It would spoil him to receive at once all that is to be his when he enters upon his father's inheritance. Because the son is in his nonage, if he were trusted with a large sum of money or the estate, he might grow licentious and waste his wealth and privileges.

You and I, if we are believers in the Lord Jesus Christ, are kings; not only sons of God but also kings who are to reign with Him forever. Why, then, are we not treated like kings? You know that in some earthly royal families it is thought best that the heir-apparent to the throne should serve his country as a soldier or a sailor so that when he comes to the throne, he may understand how to wield his scepter for the good of all classes of his subjects. So, Christian, it is with you. You are so childish at present, having only begun to learn the nature of divine things; you are so uninstructed; you know only in part, and you know that part so badly that it would not be fitting that your greatness should be revealed to you at present. You must be held back for a while till you have been better trained in the Holy Spirit's school, and then it shall appear what you shall be.

A third reason why it does not yet appear what we shall be is, I think, because *this is not the world in which the Christian is to appear in his glory*, for if he did, his glory would be lost in this world. The multitudes climbed to the tops of the trees or the roofs of the houses, where they might see Caesar or Pompey returning with the spoils of war, and the multitudes still clap their hands when a warrior has overcome his country's enemies and so become a great man. But the world cares little or nothing about self-denial, about Christian love, about holiness and devotion to Christ and His cause, yet these things are the glory of a Christian. That moral excellence, that spiritual worth that flashes from the eyes of the holy angels and of the saints in glory, is almost unappreciated here. Your Master had this glory, though it was usually veiled while He was here below, yet the people cried out, "Crucify him, crucify him" (Luke 23:21); and if you had here, to its full extent, the glory that will be revealed in you in heaven, people would say the same concerning you.

This is not the world in which you are to display your full honors. When a king is journeying through a foreign country, he does not wear his crown or the rest of his regalia. He often travels *incognito*; and even when he reaches his own country, he does not put on his royal robes for fools to admire at every village fair. He is not a puppet king, strutting upon the stage to show himself to the common people, but he reserves his grandeur for great public occasions and grand court ceremonies. In this poor sinful world, you Christians would be out of place if you could be what you shall yet be. You also must go *incognito* through this world to a large extent, but by and by, you shall take off the travel-worn garments of your earthly pilgrimage and put on your beautiful array and be manifested to the whole universe as a son or a daughter of "the King eternal, immortal, invisible" (1 Tim. 1:17).

One last reason why "it doth not yet appear what we shall be" is that *this is not the time for the display of the Christian's glory.* If I may use this expression, time is not the time for the manifestation of a Christian's glory. Eternity is to be the period for the Christian's full development and for the sinless display of his God-given glory. Here he must expect to be unknown; it is in the hereafter that he is to be discovered as a son of the great King. At present, it is with us as it is with the world during the winter. If you had not seen the miracle wrought over and over, you would not guess, when you look upon those black beds in the garden or when you walk over that snowy and frosty covering, crisp and hard beneath your feet, that the earth will yet be sown with all the colors of the rainbow and that it will be gemmed with flowers of unspeakable beauty. No, the winter is not the time when the beauty of the earth is to be best seen; and, Christian, you also must pass through your winter season. Ay, but let that wintry weather once be over, let the bleak December winds howl into your ears, let the cold and cheerless January come and go, let February also pass; and, behold, the springtime comes. I might also say that gray hairs come upon your head, like the snowdrops appear upon the earth, as the messenger of spring and of summer, and your soul shall yet blossom "with joy unspeakable and full of glory" (1 Pet. 1:8), and all the graces and excellences of the Christian shall be revealed in you.

If you stand at the seaside, you have noticed that at certain hours of the day there is a long expanse of mud or of dry sand, and it may not seem to one who sees it for the first time as though the sea had ever rolled over it or that it ever will. Ah, but "it doth not yet appear" what it will be. It is ebb tide now, but wait till the flood comes, and then you will see the whole of that black mire or that yellow sand glistening in the sunshine. So the flood of glory is rising for the believer in Christ; can you not see the breakers in the distance, the white crests of the incoming waves? God's great sea of eternity draws nearer and nearer; can you not hear the booming of that mighty flood? Soon shall your ransomed spirit float and bathe in that sea of glory, where not a single wave shall cause you a moment's grief or pain. This is not the time in which you are to be fully revealed. You are, today, like that ugly, shriveled seed; there is no beauty in it that you should desire it. But wait a little while, and when the sweetly perfumed flower shall shed its fragrance on the air and make the gazer pause to admire the matchless colors with which God has been pleased to paint it, then shall its full glory be known and seen. At present, you are in your seed stage, and your sowing time is coming. Tremble not that it is so. There will be a time for your poor flesh to sleep in the silent grave, but at the voice of the archangel and the blast of the trumpet of the resurrection, you shall arise. Just as the flower rises in spring, the dead body that was put into the tomb shall rise incorruptible in the image of the Savior.

So, you see, "it doth not yet appear what we shall be," because the Lord Jesus Christ was not fully revealed here, because we are not prepared to appear in glory, because we are not here in the midst of the men and women who should see us in our glory, and because it is not yet the right time for us thus to appear. "To every thing there is a season, and a time to every purpose under the heaven" (Eccl. 3:1), but this is not the time for the full manifestation of Christians; and therefore "it doth not yet appear what we shall be; but we know that, when he shall appear, we shall be like him, for we shall see him as he is."

"But We Know That, When He Shall Appear"

So, then, *it is quite certain that Christ will appear.* John does not stop to prove it. He speaks of it as though it were perfectly understood that Christ would again appear, and he mentions what is to be the nature of that appearing.

Christ will appear in person. This is what the two angels declared to the disciples after the Lord's ascension: "This same Jesus, which is taken up from you into heaven, shall so come in like manner as ye have seen him go into heaven" (Acts 1:11); that is, as the incarnate God He will come back from heaven.

When He comes, *He will appear full of happiness.* There will be no more sorrow to wrinkle His brow, no more furrows to be plowed on His back, no fresh wounds to be made in His hands or

His feet, no more offering of a sacrifice for sin; but He will come to rejoice with His people forever.

Further, when He comes, *He will appear in His glory*—not as the man of Nazareth, to be despised and spit upon, but as "The mighty God, The everlasting Father, The Prince of Peace" (Isa. 9:6). If any of you are tempted to ask, "When will He come?" I give you His own assurance: "Surely I come quickly"; so go your way and pray, as John did, "Even so, come, Lord Jesus" (Rev. 22:20); yet do not forget Paul's inspired sentences, "But of the times and the seasons, brethren, ye have no need that I write unto you. For yourselves know perfectly that the day of the Lord so cometh as a thief in the night. For when they shall say, Peace and safety; then sudden destruction cometh upon them, as travail upon a woman with child; and they shall not escape" (1 Thess. 5:1–3). Christ is coming, literally coming—not figuratively, but literally, actually, really. He is coming in glory, to dwell in the midst of His saints forever. This is our blessed hope: "the glorious appearing of the great God and our Saviour Jesus Christ; who gave himself for us, that he might redeem us from all iniquity, and purify unto himself a peculiar people, zealous of good works" (Titus 2:13–14).

We Shall Be Like Him

There are other passages in God's Word where we are distinctly told that Jesus' manifestation will be coincident with our manifestation. Here, we are told that "when he shall appear, we shall be like him"; and the reason given for this is, "for we shall see him as he is." While considering the text, let us meditate upon this great truth: "We shall be like him."

This glorious assurance that we shall be like Christ can easily seem too good to be true. Yet it is true that *we are to be like Christ*, first, *as to our body*. Here, we are like the first Adam—of the earth, earthy. But we shall one day have a body like that of the second Adam, a heavenly body like Christ's. Like the first Adam, we are mortal now; like the second Adam, the day shall come when we will be immortal. Christ's body is not now subject to any pains or to any decay or disease; neither shall our body be. It is quite true that "flesh and blood cannot inherit the kingdom of God" (1 Cor. 15:50), yet it will be this very body of ours that will inherit the kingdom of God, only that which is corruptible in it, that which is mere flesh and blood, will then have been removed. As the apostle Paul writes to the Corinthians in that wonderful chapter about the resurrection: "It is sown a natural body: it is raised a spiritual body" (1 Cor. 15:44). It is "a spiritual body" that the Lord Jesus Christ has today. I cannot imagine how glorious the Savior is in heaven, but I always think of Him, even when He was upon this earth, as being far fairer than any artist ever depicted Him. I have gazed a long while upon many paintings of Christ, but I have never yet seen one that appeared to be equal to my ideal of the Savior. I have looked, and I have said, "Oh, no! He was far fairer than that; there must have been more beauty in His face than even that great master has portrayed."

If that is true concerning Him as He was when among the sons of men, how true it must be concerning Him as He is now! He is fairer than all the fair spirits that surround the heavenly throne. He is "the rose of Sharon, and the lily of the valleys" (Song of Sol. 2:1). Among the shining seraphim and cherubim, none can be compared with Him, and we are to be like Him. Whatever are the characteristics of the Savior's glorified body, they are to be the characteristics of your body also. You are to have an immortal body, a spiritual body, a body incapable of pain and suffering and decay, a body that shall be suited to your emancipated spirit. I expect that our new bodies will have a far wider range of mobility than this limited earthly sphere, perhaps allowing us to fly as swiftly as light from world to world, or possibly having the power even to outrun the lightning's flash. I do not know how wondrous Christ's glorified body is, but I do "know that, when he shall appear, we shall be like him [even in body]; for we shall see him as he is."

But far more important than that, *we shall also be* like *Christ in soul*. Have the eyes of your spiritual understanding or sanctified imagination ever looked upon Christ's spotless soul, that perfect spirit in which no one power or passion was too prominent or predominant but in which His whole being was beautifully molded and rounded according to the perfect pattern of moral excellence and beauty? Now, beloved, you are to be just like that, not quick in temper, as perhaps you now are, but meek and lowly as He was, not haughty and prone to pride but humble and gentle as He was, not selfish and self-seeking but as loving and as tender to others as He was; in fact, perfection's own self.

What a joy it is to us to know that we shall be like Him! This blessed truth is enough to make you stand up or even leap in the exuberance of your joy. I have heard of our enthusiastic Welsh friends dancing during some of their preachers' sermons, and if this is the truth that makes them dance, who can wonder at it? "We shall be like him"—like Him in soul, with no more weaknesses of temper or sloth or undue haste. Our human nature shall be rid of all its rags, and we shall be perfect, even as our Father in heaven is perfect. Oh, that the blessed day had already come, and that we were like our Lord! But "we shall be like him; for we shall see him as he is."

I should also add that *we shall be like Christ* not only in body and in soul but *also in condition*. We shall be with Him where He is, and we shall be as happy as He is, as far as our capacity for happiness goes. We shall be crowned even as He is crowned, and we shall sit upon thrones even as He sits upon His Father's throne. He shall lead us to living fountains of water and be our constant companion, never going away from us again. He shall call us His brethren, and we shall share in His honor and glory. The joy of that we shall partake shall be His joy, and it will be in us that our joy may be full. O Christian, think lofty thoughts concerning your Lord in glory, and remember that you shall be like Him!

For We Shall See Him As He Is

How is it that we shall be like Him? Partly, *by reflection*, "for we shall see him as he is." When a man looks into a bright mirror, it makes him also bright, for it throws its own light upon his face; this is only according to the laws of light. And in a much more wonderful fashion, when we look at Christ, who is all brightness, He throws some of His brightness upon us. When Moses went up into the mount to commune with God, his face shone because he had received a reflection of God's glory upon his face. He had looked into the blazing light of deity, as far as a created eye could look there, and that light was so brilliantly reflected in his own face that Aaron and the people were afraid to draw near him, and he had to cover his face with a veil while he spoke to them.

Further, beloved, we get to be like Christ by seeing Him *in type and symbol*, as through a glass darkly. The Lord's Supper is one of the glasses; believers' baptism is another; the preaching of the Word is another; the Bible itself is another of these glasses. It is only a partial reflection of Christ that we get from all these glasses, yet, as we look at it, as Paul writes to the Corinthians, "We all, with open face beholding as in a glass the glory of the Lord, are changed into the same image from glory to glory, even as by the Spirit of the Lord" (2 Cor. 3:18).

But if there is such a sanctifying influence about the very reflection of Jesus Christ, *what a wondrous power it must have upon us when we see Him as He is!* When we shall gaze upon Him with unveiled vision and see Him as He is, do you wonder that John says that at this moment "we shall be like him; for we shall see him as he is"? Oh, that amazing sight, that unique sight of Jesus as He is! It would be worth dying a thousand painful deaths to get one brief glimpse of Him as He is. I do not think that Rutherford exaggerated when he talked of swimming through seven hells to get at Christ if he could not get at Him any other way. A distant view of Christ, as we have seen Him "leaping upon the mountains, skipping upon the hills" (Song of Sol. 2:8), has so ravished our souls that we have scarcely known whether we have been in the body or out of the body. When we have heard His voice, we have longed to be with Him. What must it be like to be there? What must it be to see our Savior as He is?

In some of the houses not far from our church, I have noticed some small songbirds in cages in which there were tufts of grass or small branches of trees as perches for the poor prisoners. Yet those birds were singing away merrily. I suppose that grass and those fragments of trees were meant to remind them, in this great, dirty, smoky city, that there are green fields and wide forests somewhere. I thought, as I looked upon them, "Ah, you poor birds are very like what I myself am! My Master has put me in a little cage and told me to remain here for a while; and He has given me my little tuft of grass as an earnest of my inheritance in the sweet fields beyond the swelling flood. He graciously sends me a few comforts on the way. Ah, but that poor little tuft of grass! What is it in comparison with the fields and the hedges that are the proper home of the songbirds that have their liberty?

Christian, you do not know what it will be for you to have your cage door opened, that you may fly away to that blessed land where the true birds of Paradise forever warble from their joyful throats the loudest praises to the great King who has set them free forever. Let us begin the music here; let us try even now to anticipate that happy day.

O brethren, we may well stand fast, since we have infinite power at our backs. The Lord is with us with all His energy, even with His all-conquering strength, that shall yet subdue all His foes. Do not let us imagine that any enemy can be too strong for Christ's arm. If He is able to subdue all things to Himself, He can certainly bear us through all opposition. One glance of His eye may wither all opposers, or better still, one word from His lips may turn them into friends.

Chapter Eleven

Stand Fast

For our conversation is in heaven; from whence also we look for the Saviour, the Lord Jesus Christ: who shall change our vile body, that it may be fashioned like unto his glorious body, according to the working whereby he is able even to subdue all things unto himself. Therefore, my brethren dearly beloved and longed for, my joy and crown, so stand fast in the Lord, my dearly beloved.
—Philippians 3:20–4:1

EVERY DOCTRINE OF THE WORD of God has its practical bearing. As each tree bears seed after its kind, so does every truth of God bring forth practical virtues. Hence, you find the apostle Paul very full of *therefores*—his therefores being the conclusions drawn from certain statements of divine truth. I marvel that our excellent translators should have divided the argument from the conclusion by making a new chapter where there is little reason for it.

I have often written on the most sure and certain resurrection of our Lord Jesus: now there is a practical force in that truth, that constitutes part of what is meant by "the power of his resurrection" (Phil. 3:10). Since the Lord has risen and will surely come a second time and will raise the bodies of His people at His coming, there is something to wait for, and a grand reason for steadfastness while we wait. We are looking for the coming of our Lord and Savior Jesus Christ from heaven, and that He shall fashion anew the body of our humiliation that it may be conformed to the body of His glory; therefore, let us stand fast in the position that will secure us this honor. Let us keep our posts until the coming of the great Captain shall release the sentinels.

The glorious resurrection will abundantly repay us for all the toil and travail we may have to undergo in the battle for the Lord. The glory to be revealed even now casts a light upon our path and causes sunshine within our hearts. The hope of this happiness makes us even now strong in the Lord and in the power of His might.

Paul was deeply anxious that those in whom he had been the means of kindling the heavenly hope might be preserved faithful until the coming of Christ. He trembled lest any of them should seem to draw back and prove traitors to their Lord. He dreaded lest he should lose what he hoped he had gained by their turning aside from the faith. Hence, he beseeched them to "stand fast." He expressed in the sixth verse of the first chapter his conviction that He who had begun a good work in them would perform it, but his intense love made him exhort them, saying, "Stand fast in the Lord, my dearly beloved." By such exhortations, final persever- ance is promoted and secured.

Paul has fought bravely; and in the case of the Philippian con- verts, he believes that he has secured the victory, and he fears lest it should yet be lost. He reminds me of the death of that British hero Wolfe, who on the heights of Quebec received a mortal wound. It was just at the moment when the enemy fled, and when he knew that they were running, a smile was on his face, and he said, "Hold me up. Let not my brave soldiers see me drop. The day is ours. Oh, do keep it!" His sole anxiety was to make the victory sure.

Thus warriors die, and thus Paul lived. His very soul seems to cry, "We have won the day. Oh, do keep it!" O my beloved readers, I entreat you to "stand fast in the Lord." In your case, also, the day is won, but oh, do keep it! May God the Holy Spirit write it on your hearts! Having done all things well, I entreat you to obey the injunction of Jude to "keep yourselves in the love of God" (vs. 21) and to join with me in adoring Him who alone is able to keep us from falling and to present us faultless before His presence with exceeding great joy (Jude 24). Unto Him be glory forever. Amen.

Having Begun Well

It is very important indeed that we should begin well. The start is not everything, but it is a great deal. An old proverb says that "well begun is half done," and it is certainly so in the things of God. It is vital to enter in at the narrow gate, to start on the heavenly journey from the right point. I have no doubt that many slips and falls and apostasies occur among professing believers because they were not right at first; the foundation was always upon the sand, and when the house came down at last, it was no more than might have been expected. A flaw in the foundation is pretty sure to be followed by a crack in the superstructure. Do see to it that you lay a good foundation. It is even better to have no repentance than a repentance that needs to be repented of; better to have no faith than a false faith; better to make no profession of religion than to make an untruthful one.

God give us grace that we may not make a mistake in learning the alphabet of godliness, or else in all our learning we shall blunder on and increase in error. We should early learn the difference between grace and merit, between the purpose of God and the will of man, between trust in God and confidence in the flesh. If we do not start correctly, the further we go, the further we shall be from our desired end, and the more thoroughly in the wrong shall we find ourselves. Yes, it is of prime importance that our new birth and our first love should be genuine beyond all question.

The only position, however, in which we can begin aright is to be "in the Lord." This is the place to begin so that we may safely go on. This is the essential point. It is a very good thing for Christians to be in the church, but if you are in the church before you are in the Lord, you are out of place. It is a good thing to be engaged in holy work, but if you are in holy work before you are in the Lord, you will have no heart for it, neither will the Lord accept it. It is not essential that you should be in this church or in that church, but it is essential that you should be "in the Lord."

What is it to be "in the Lord"? Well, we *are in the Lord vitally and evidently when we fly to the Lord Jesus by repentance and faith* and make Him to be our refuge and hiding place. Is it so with you? Have you fled out of self? Are you trusting in the Lord alone? Have you come to Calvary and beheld your Savior? As the doves build their nests in the rock, have you thus made your home in Jesus? There is no shelter for a guilty soul but in Jesus' wounded side. Have you come there?

Next, these people, in addition to having fled to Christ for refuge, were now *in Christ as to their daily life*. They had heard Him say, "Abide in me" (John 15:4), and therefore they remained in the daily enjoyment of Him, in reliance upon Him, in obedience to Him, and in the earnest copying of His example. They were Christians, that is to say, persons upon whom was named the name of Christ. They were endeavoring to realize the power of His death and resurrection as a sanctifying influence, killing their sins and fostering their virtues. They were laboring to reproduce His image in themselves so that they might bring glory to His name. Their lives were spent within the circle of their Savior's influence.

This expression is very short but very full—"in Christ." Does it not mean that we are in Christ as the birds are in the air that buoys them up and enables them to fly? Are we not in Christ as the fish are in the sea? *Our Lord has become our element*, vital and all surrounding. Has Jesus brought you into His green pastures? Then lie down in them. Go no further, for you will never fare better. Stay with your Lord, however long the night, for only in Him have you hope of morning.

You see, then, that these people were where they should be—in the Lord—and that this was the reason the apostle took such delight in them. Kindly read the first verse of the fourth chapter and see how he loves them and joys over them. He heaps up titles of love! Some dip their morsel in vinegar, but Paul's words were saturated with honey. His love was real and fervent. The very heart of Paul is written out large in this verse—"Therefore, my brethren dearly beloved and longed for, my joy and crown, so stand fast in the Lord, my dearly beloved." Because they were in Christ, therefore first of all they were Paul's *brethren*. This was a new relationship, not earthly but heavenly.

What did this Jew from Tarsus know about the Philippians? Many of them were Gentiles. Time was when he would have called them dogs and despised them as the uncircumcised, but now he calls them, "my brethren." That poor word has become very trite. We talk of brethren without particularly much of brotherly love; but true brothers have a love for one another that is very unselfish and admirable, and so there is between real Christians a brotherhood that they will neither disown nor dissemble nor forget.

It is said of our Lord, for this cause He "is not ashamed to call them brethren" (Heb. 2:11), and surely they need never be ashamed to call one another brethren. Paul, at any rate, looks at the jailer, that jailer who had set his feet in the stocks, and he looks at the jailer's family, and at Lydia, and many others, in fact, at the whole company that he had gathered at Philippi, and he salutes them lovingly as "my brethren." Their names were written in the same family register because they were in Christ and therefore had one Father in heaven.

Next, the apostle calls them "my *dearly beloved*." The verse almost begins with this word, and it quite finishes with it. The repetition makes it mean "my doubly dear ones." Such is the love that every true servant of Christ will have for those who have been brought to the faith of Christ by his means. Oh, yes, if you are in Christ, His ministers must love you. How could there be a lack of affection in our hearts toward you, since we have been the means of bringing you to Jesus? Without empty talk or display, we call you our "dearly beloved."

Then the apostle calls them his "*longed for*," that is, his most desired ones. He first desired to see them converted and baptized; then he desired to see them exhibiting all the graces of Christians. When he saw holiness in them, he desired to visit them and commune with them. Their constant kindness created in him a strong desire to speak with them face to face. He loved them and desired their company because they were in Christ. So he speaks of them as those for whom he longed. His delight was in thinking of them and in hoping to visit them.

Then he adds, "my joy and crown." Paul had been the means of their salvation, and when he thought of that blessed result, he never regretted all that he had suffered: his persecutions among the Gentiles seemed light indeed, since these priceless souls were his reward. Though he was nothing but a poor prisoner of Christ, yet he talks in a royal style: they are his crown. They were his *stephanos*, or crown given as a reward for his life race. This among the Greeks was usually a wreath of flowers placed around the victor's brow.

Paul's crown would never fade. He writes as he felt the amaranth around his temples; even now he looks upon the Philippians as his garland of honor: they were his joy and his crown. Paul anticipated, I do not doubt, that throughout eternity it would be a part of his heaven to see them amid their blessedness and to know that he had helped to bring them to that bliss by leading them to Christ.

O beloved, it is indeed our highest joy that we have not run in vain, neither labored in vain. You who have been snatched as "a brand plucked out of the fire" (Zech. 3:2) and are now living to the praise of our Lord Jesus Christ, you are our prize, our crown, our joy.

Stand Fast

Paul entreated them to stand fast: "so stand fast in the Lord, my dearly beloved." The beginning of religion is not the whole of it. You must not suppose that the sum of godliness is contained within the experience of a day or two or a week or a few months or even a few years. Precious are the feelings that attend conversion, but dream not that repentance and faith are for a season and then all is over and done with.

I am afraid there are some who secretly say, "I have experienced the necessary change, I have been to see the elders and the pastor, I have been baptized and received into the church, and now all is right forever." That is a false view of your condition. In conversion, you have started in the race, and you must run to the end of the course. In your confession of Christ, you have carried your tools into the vineyard, but the day's work now begins. Remember, "He that shall endure unto the end, the same shall be saved" (Mark 13:13). Godliness is a lifelong business. The working out of the salvation that the Lord Himself works in you is not a matter of certain hours and of a limited period of life. Salvation is unfolded throughout all our sojourn here. We continue to repent and to believe, and even the process of our conversion continues as we are changed more and more into the image of our Lord. Final perseverance is the necessary evidence of genuine conversion.

In proportion as we rejoice over converts we feel an intense bitterness when any turn out to be merely temporary followers. We sigh over the seed that springs up so quickly but withers so soon, for it has neither root nor depth of earth. For one reason and another, they went back: "They went out from us, but they were not of us; for if they had been of us, they would no doubt have continued with us: but they went out, that they might be made manifest that they were not all of us" (1 John 2:19).

Our churches suffer most seriously from the great numbers who drop out of their ranks and either go back to the world or else must be pursuing a very secret and solitary path in their way to heaven, for we hear no more of them. Our joy is turned to disappointment, our crown of laurel becomes a circle of faded leaves, and we are weary at the remembrance of it. With what earnestness, therefore, would we say to you who are beginning the race, "Continue in your course. Turn not aside, neither slacken your running, till you have won the prize!"

I heard an expression yesterday that pleased me much. I spoke about the difficulty of keeping on. "Yes," answered my friend, "and it is harder still to keep on keeping on." So it is. There is the pinch. I have known many people who are wonders at the start, but then there is no stay in them: they soon lose breath. The difference between the spurious and the real Christian lies in this staying power. The real Christian has a life within him that can never die, an incorruptible seed that lives and abides forever, but the spurious Christian begins after a fashion but ends almost as soon as he begins. He is esteemed a saint but turns out a hypocrite. He makes a fair show for a while, but soon he quits the way of holiness. God save you, dear friend, from anything that looks like apostasy. Hence, I would with all my might press upon you these two most weighty words: "Stand fast."

I will put the exhortation thus—"Stand fast *doctrinally*." In this age, all the ships in the waters are pulling up their anchors and are drifting with the tide, being driven about with every wind. It is your wisdom to put down more anchors. I have taken the precaution to cast four anchors out of the stern as well as to see that the great bower anchor is in its proper place. I will not budge an inch from the old doctrine for any man.

Now that the hurricane is triumphant over many a bowing wall and tottering fence, those who are built upon the one foundation must prove its value by standing fast. We will hearken to no teaching but that of the Lord Jesus. If you see a truth to be in God's Word, grasp it by your faith, and if it is unpopular, clasp it to you as with hooks of steel. If you are despised as a fool for holding it, hold it the more. Like an oak, take deeper root, because the winds would tear you from your place. Defy reproach and ridicule, and you have already vanquished it.

Stand fast, like the British troops in the olden times. When fierce assaults were made upon them, every man seemed transformed to rock. We might have wandered from the ranks a little in more peaceful times, to look after the fascinating flowers that grow on every side of our march; but now that we know that the enemy surrounds us, we keep strictly to the line of march and tolerate no roaming. The watchword of the host of God just now is—"Stand fast!" Hold to the faith once delivered to the saints. Hold fast the form of sound words and deviate not one jot or tittle from it. Doctrinally stand fast!

Practically, also, abide firm in the right, the true, the holy. This is of the utmost importance. The barriers are broken down for those who would commingle the church and the world. I repeat to you this word: "Come out from among them, and be ye separate, saith the Lord, and touch not the unclean thing" (2 Cor. 6:17). Write "holiness unto the Lord" not only on your altars but also upon the bells of the horses (Zech. 14:20). Let everything be done as before the living God. Do all things unto holiness and edification. Strive together to maintain the purity of the disciples of Christ, and take up your cross and go without the camp bearing His reproach.

If you have already stood apart in your decision for the Lord, continue to do so. Stand fast. In nothing moved by the laxity of the age, in nothing affected by the current modern opinion, say to yourself, "I will do as Christ bids me to the utmost of my ability. I will follow the Lamb wherever He goes." In these times of worldliness, impurity, self-indulgence, and error, it becomes the Christian to keep his feet and his garments clean from the pollution that lies all around him. We must be more precise than we have been. Oh, for grace to stand fast!

Mind also that you stand fast *experientially*. Pray that your inward experience may be a close bonding to your Master. Do not go astray from His presence. Neither climb with those who dream of perfection in the flesh, nor grovel with those who doubt the possibility of present salvation. Take the Lord Jesus Christ to be your sole treasure, and let your heart be ever with Him.

Stand fast in faith in His atonement, in confidence in His divinity, in assurance of His second coming. I desire to know within my soul the power of His resurrection and to have unbroken fellowship with Him. In communion with the Father and the Son, let us stand fast. He shall fare well whose heart and soul, affections and understanding are wrapped up in Christ Jesus and in none beside. Concerning your inward life, your secret prayer, your walk with God, here is the watchword of the day—"Stand fast."

Next, stand fast *without wavering in your trust*. Permit no doubt to worry you. So commit yourself into His hands that you are as sure of your salvation as of your existence. The blood of Jesus Christ this day cleanses us from all sin; His righteousness covers us, and His life quickens us into newness of life. Tolerate no doubt, mistrust, suspicion, or misgiving. Believe in Christ up to the hilt. As for myself, I will yield to be lost forever if Jesus does not save me. I will have no other string to my bow, no second door of hope or way of retreat. I could risk a thousand souls on my Lord's truth and feel no risk. Stand fast, without wishing for another trust and without wavering in the trust you have.

Moreover, stand fast *without wandering into sin.* You are tempted this way and that way: stand fast. Inward passions rise, lusts of the flesh rebel, the devil hurls his fearful suggestions, the men of your own household tempt you: stand fast. Only so will you be preserved from the torrents of iniquity. Keep close to the example and spirit of your Master, and having done all, still stand.

I must also tell you to stand fast *without wearying.* You are a little tired. Never mind, take a little rest and brush up again. "Oh," you say, "this toil is so monotonous." Do it better, and that will be a change. Your Savior endured His life and labor without this complaint, for zeal had eaten Him up. "Alas," you cry, "I cannot see results." Never mind; wait for results, even as the farmer waits for the precious fruits of the earth. "Oh, sir, I plod along and make no progress." Never mind, you are a poor judge of your own success. Work on, for in due season, you shall reap if you faint not. Practice perseverance.

Remember that if you have the work of faith and the labor of love, you must complete the trio by adding the patience of hope. You cannot do without this last. "Be ye stedfast, unmoveable, always abounding in the work of the Lord, forasmuch as ye know that your labour is not in vain in the Lord" (1 Cor. 15:58). I am reminded of Sir Christopher Wren when he cleared away old St. Paul's to make room for his splendid building. He was compelled to use battering rams upon the massive walls. The workmen kept on battering and battering. An enormous force was brought to bear upon the walls for days and nights, but it did not appear to have made the least impression upon the ancient masonry. Yet the great architect knew what he was at and told the workers to keep on incessantly. The ram fell again and again upon the rocky wall, till at length the whole mass was disintegrating and coming apart, and finally each stroke began to tell. At a blow it reeled, at another it quivered, at another it moved visibly, at another it fell over amid clouds of dust.

These last strokes did the work. Do you think so? No, it was the sum of blows, the first as truly as the last. Keep on with the battering ram. I hope to keep on until I die. And, mark you, I may die and may not see the errors of the hour totter to their fall, but I shall be perfectly content to sleep in Christ, for I have a sure expectation that this work will succeed in the end. I shall be happy to have done my share of the work even if I personally see little apparent result. Lord, let Your work appear to Your servants, and we will be content that Your glory should be reserved for our children. Stand fast in incessant labors, for the end is sure.

And then, in addition to standing fast in that respect, stand fast *without warping*. Timber, when it is rather green, is apt to warp this way or that. The spiritual weather is very bad just now for green wood; it is one day damp with superstition, and another day it is parched with skepticism. Rationalism and ritualism are both at work. I pray that you may not warp. Keep straight; keep to the truth, the whole truth, and nothing but the truth, for in the Master's name we bid you "stand fast in the Lord."

Stand fast, for there is great need. Many walk of whom I have told you often and now tell you even weeping, that they are the enemies of the cross of Christ.

The Best Motives for Standing Fast

Paul says, "Stand fast *because of your citizenship*." Read the twentieth verse: "For our citizenship is in heaven." Now, if you are what you profess to be, if you are in Christ, you are a citizen of the New Jerusalem. Men should behave themselves according to their citizenship and not dishonor their city.

When a man was a citizen of Athens in the olden time, he felt it incumbent upon himself to be brave. The Persian king Xerxes said, "These Athenians are not ruled by kings. How will they fight?" "No," said one, "but every man respects the law, and each man is ready to die for his country." Xerxes soon had to know that the same obedience and respect of law ruled the Spartans and that these, because they were of Sparta, were all brave as lions. He sends word to Leonidas and his little troop to give up their arms. "Come and take them" was the courageous reply. The Persian king had myriads of soldiers with him, while Leonidas had only three hundred Spartans at his side, yet they kept the pass, and it cost the eastern despot many thousands of men to force a passage. The sons of Sparta died rather than desert their post. Every citizen of Sparta felt that he must stand fast: it was not for such a man as he to yield.

We must not yield, we dare not yield, if we are of the city of the great King. The martyrs cry to us to stand fast; the cloud of witnesses bending from their thrones above beseech us to stand fast; yea, all the hosts of the shining ones cry to us, "Stand fast." Stand fast for God and the truth and holiness, and let no man take your crown.

The next argument that Paul used was *their outlook*. "Our conversation is in heaven; from whence also we look for the Saviour, the Lord Jesus Christ." Brethren, Jesus is coming. He is even now on the way. You have heard our tidings till you scarcely credit us, but the word is true, and it will surely be fulfilled before long. The Lord is coming indeed. He first promised to come to die, and He kept His word. He now promises to come to reign, and you may be sure that He will keep His meeting with His people. Ears of faith can hear the sound of His chariot wheels; every moment of time, every event of providence is bringing Him nearer. Blessed are those servants who shall not be sleeping when He comes or wandering from their posts of duty; happy shall they be whom their Lord shall find faithfully watching and standing fast in that great day!

To us, beloved, He is coming, not as Judge and Destroyer but as *Savior*. We look for the Savior, the Lord Jesus Christ. Now, if we look for Him, let us "stand fast." There must be no going into sin, no forsaking the fellowship with other believers, no leaving the truth, no trying to play fast and loose with godliness. Let us stand so fast in singleness of heart that whenever Jesus comes, we shall be able to say, "Welcome, welcome, Son of God!"

Sometimes I wait through the weary years with great comfort. There was a ship some time ago outside a certain harbor. A heavy sea made the ship roll fearfully. A dense fog blotted out all buoys and lights. The captain never left the wheel. He could not tell his way into the harbor, and no pilot could get out to him for a long time. Eager passengers urged him to be courageous and make a dash for the harbor. He said, "No, it is not my duty to run so great a risk. A pilot is required here, and I will wait for one if I wait a week."

The truest courage is that which can bear to be charged with cowardice. To wait is much wiser than, when you cannot hear the foghorn and have no pilot, yet you steam on and wreck your vessel on the rocks. Our prudent captain waited his time, and at last he detected the pilot's boat coming to him over the boiling sea. When the pilot was at his work, the captain's anxious waiting was over.

The Church is like that vessel. She is pitched to and fro in the storm and the dark, and the Pilot has not yet come. The weather is very threatening. All around, the darkness hangs like a pall. But Jesus will come, walking on the water, before long; He will bring us safe to the desired haven. Let us wait with patience. Stand fast! Stand fast! Jesus is coming, and in Him is our sure hope.

Further, there was another motive. *There was an expectation.* "He shall change our vile body," or rather, "body of our humiliation." Only think of it, dear friend! No more heart attacks or heartaches, no more feebleness and fainting, no more inward tumors or disease; but the Lord shall transfigure this body of our humiliation into the likeness of the body of His glory. Our frame is now made up of decaying substances, it is of the earth earthy. "So to the dust return we must." This body groans, suffers, becomes diseased, and dies: blessed be God, it shall be wonderfully changed, and then there shall be no more death, neither sorrow nor crying, neither shall there be any more pain.

The natural appetites of this body beget sad tendencies to sin, and in this respect it is a "vile body." It shall not always be so! The great change will deliver it from all that is gross and carnal. It shall be pure as the Lord's body! Whatever the body of Christ is now, our body is to be like it. We are to have a real, corporeal body as He had for substance and reality; and like His body, it will be full of beauty, full of health and strength; it will enjoy peculiar immunities from evil and special adaptations for good.

That is what is going to happen to me and to you; therefore, let us stand fast. Let us not willfully throw away our prospects of glory and immortality. What! Relinquish resurrection? Relinquish glory? Relinquish likeness to the risen Lord? O God, save us from such a terrible piece of apostasy! Save us from such immeasurable folly! Suffer us not to turn our backs in the day of battle, since that would be to turn our backs from the crown of life that never fades away.

Finally, the apostle urges us to stand fast because of *our resources.* Somebody may ask, "How can this body of ours be transformed and transfigured until it becomes like the body of Christ?" I cannot tell you anything about the process; it will all be accomplished in the twinkling of an eye, at the last trumpet. But I can tell you by what power it will be accomplished. The omnipotent Lord will lay bare His arm and exercise His might "according to the working whereby he is able even to subdue all things unto himself."

O brethren, we may well stand fast, since we have infinite power at our backs. The Lord is with us with all His energy, even with His all-conquering strength, that shall yet subdue all His foes. Do not let us imagine that any enemy can be too strong for Christ's arm. If He is able to subdue all things to Himself, He can certainly bear us through all opposition. One glance of His eye may wither all opposers, or better still, one word from His lips may turn them into friends.

The army of the Lord is strong in reserves. These reserves have never yet been fully called out. We who are in the field are only a small squadron, holding the fort, but our Lord has at His back ten thousand times ten thousand who will carry war into the enemy's camp. When the Captain of our salvation comes to the front, He will bring His heavenly legions with Him. Our business is to watch until He appears upon the scene, for when He comes, His infinite resources will be put in marching order.

I like that speech of Wellington (who was so calm amid the roar of Waterloo) when an officer sent word, "Tell the Commander-in-Chief that he must move me, I cannot hold my position any longer, my numbers are so thinned." "Tell him," said the great general, "he *must* hold his place. Every Englishman today must die where he stands, or else win the victory." The officer read the command to stand, and he did stand till the trumpet sounded victory.

And so it is now. We must die where we are rather than yield to the enemy. If Jesus tarries, we must not desert our posts. Wellington knew that the heads of the Prussian columns would soon be visible, coming in to insure the victory; and so by faith we can perceive the legions of our Lord approaching: in serried ranks His angels fly through the opening heaven. The air is teeming with them. I hear their silver trumpets. Behold, He comes with clouds! When He comes He will abundantly recompense all who stood fast amid the rage of battle. Let us sing, "Hold the fort, for I am coming."

*H*ave you caught the idea, and do you see there afar off upon the lofty top, not everlasting snows but a pure crystal tableland, crowned with a gorgeous city, the metropolis of God, the royal palace of Jesus the King. The sun is eclipsed by the light that shines from the top of this mountain; the moon ceases from her brightness, for there is now no night: but this one hill, lifted up on high, illuminates the atmosphere, and the nations of them that are saved are walking in its light. The hill of Zion has now outsoared all others, and all the mountains and hills of the earth are become as nothing before her. This is the magnificent picture of the text. I do not know that in all the compass of poetry there is an idea so massive and stupendous as this—a mountain heaving, expanding, swelling, growing, till all the high hills become absorbed, and what was but a little rising ground before becomes a hill the top of which reaches to the seventh heavens. Now we have here a picture of what the Church is to be.

Chapter Twelve

A Vision of the Latter-day Glories

And it shall come to pass in the last days, that the mountain of the LORD's house shall be established in the top of the mountains, and shall be exalted above the hills; and all nations shall flow unto it—Isaiah 2:2 and Micah 4:1.

THE PROPHETS OF GOD were anciently called seers, for they were given a supernatural sight that could pierce through the gloom of the future and behold the things that God has ordained for the last times. They frequently described what they saw with spiritual eyes after the form or fashion of something that could be seen by the eye of nature. The vision was so substantial that they could picture it in words, so that we also may behold in open vision the glorious things that they beheld after a supernatural sort.

Let us imagine Isaiah as he stood upon Mount Zion. He looked about him and there were the mountains that are round about Jerusalem far outvying it in height but yielding to Zion in glory. Dearer to his soul than even the snow-capped glories of Lebanon that glittered afar off was that little hill of Zion, for there upon its summit stood the temple, the shrine of the living God, the place of his delight, the home of song, the house of sacrifice, the great gathering place where the tribes went up to serve Jehovah. Standing at the gate of that glorious temple that had been piled by the matchless art of Solomon, Isaiah looked into the future and he saw, with tear-ful eye, the structure burned with fire; he beheld it cast down and the plow driven over its foundations. He saw the people carried away into Babylon and the nation cast off for a season.

Looking once more through the glass, Isaiah beheld the temple rising from its ashes, with glory outwardly diminished, but really increased. He saw on till he beheld the Messiah Himself in the form of a little babe carried into the second temple; he saw Him there, and he rejoiced; but before he had time for gladness, his eye glanced onward to the cross, where he saw the Messiah nailed to the tree; he beheld His back plowed and mangled with the whip. "Surely he hath borne our griefs, and carried our sorrows," said the prophet (Isa. 53:4), and he paused awhile to bemoan the bleeding Prince of the House of David. His eye was now doomed to a long and bitter weeping, for he saw the invading hosts of the Romans setting up the standard of desolation in the city. He saw the holy city burned with fire and utterly destroyed. His spirit was almost melted in him. But once more he flew through time with eagle's wing and scanned futurity with eagle eye; he soared aloft in imag-ination and began to sing of the last days—the end of dispen-sations and of time. He saw Messiah once again on earth. He saw that little hill of Zion rising to the clouds—reaching to heaven itself. He beheld the New Jerusalem descending from above, God dwelling among men, and all the nations flowing to the tabernacle of the Most High God, where they paid Him holy worship.

We shall not, with Isaiah, look through all the dim vista of Zion's tribulations. We will leave the avenue of troubles and of tri-als through which the Church *has* passed and *is to* pass, and we will come by faith to the last days; and may God help us while we indulge in a glorious vision of that which is to be, when "the mountain of the LORD's house shall be established in the top of the mountains, and shall be exalted above the hills; and all nations shall flow unto it." The prophet saw two things in the vision. He saw *the mountain exalted*, and he beheld *the nations flowing to it*. Now will you use your imagination for a moment, for there is a picture here that I can scarcely compare to anything. In the present instance, you will not be able to outstrip the reality, however high you may endeavor to soar, for that which is in our text will cer-tainly be greater than that which I can state or that which you may be able to conceive.

See the Mountain Exalted

Transport yourself for a moment to the foot of Mount Zion. As you stand there, you observe that it is but a very little hill. Bashan is far loftier, and Carmel and Sharon excel it. As for Lebanon, Zion is but a hill compared with it. If you think for a moment of the Alps or of the loftier Andes or of the yet mightier Himalayas, this Mount Zion seems to be a very little hill, a mere molehill—insignificant, despicable, and obscure. Stand there for a moment until the Spirit of God touches your eye, and you shall see this hill begin to grow. Up it mounts, with the temple on its summit, till it outreaches Tabor. Onward it grows, till Carmel with its perpetual green is left behind, and Salmon with its everlasting snow sinks before it. Onward still it grows, till the snowy peaks of Lebanon are eclipsed. Still onward mounts the hill, drawing with its mighty roots other mountains and hills into its fabric; and onward it rises, till piercing the clouds it reaches above the Alps. Onward still, it rises till the Himalayas seem to be sucked into its foundations and the greatest mountains of the earth appear to be but as the roots that strike out from the side of the eternal hill. And there it rises till you can scarcely see the top, as infinitely above all the higher mountains of the world as they are above the valleys.

Have you caught the idea, and do you see there afar off upon the lofty top, not everlasting snows but a pure crystal tableland, crowned with a gorgeous city, the metropolis of God, the royal palace of Jesus the King. The sun is eclipsed by the light that shines from the top of this mountain; the moon ceases from her brightness, for there is now no night: but this one hill, lifted up on high, illuminates the atmosphere, and the nations of them that are saved are walking in its light. The hill of Zion has now outsoared all others, and all the mountains and hills of the earth are become as nothing before her. This is the magnificent picture of the text. I do not know that in all the compass of poetry there is an idea so massive and stupendous as this—a mountain heaving, expanding, swelling, growing, till all the high hills become absorbed, and what was but a little rising ground before becomes a hill the top of which reaches to the seventh heavens. Now we have here a picture of what the Church is to be.

Of old, the Church was like Mount Zion, a very little hill. What did the nations of the earth see when they looked upon it?—a humble man with twelve disciples. But that little hill grew, and some thousands were baptized in the name of Christ; it grew again and became mighty. The stone cut out of the mountain without hands began to break in pieces kingdoms, and now at this day the hill of Zion stands a lofty hill. But still compared with the colossal systems of idolatry, she is but small. The Hindu and the Chinese turn to our religion and say, "It is an infant of yesterday; ours is the religion of ages." The Easterns compare Christianity to the fog that creeps along the lowlands, but their systems they imagine to be like the Alps, outsoaring the heavens in height. Ah, but we reply to this, "Your mountain crumbles and your hill dissolves, but our hill of Zion has been growing, and strange to say, it has life within its being, and grow on it *shall*, grow on it *must*, till all the systems of idolatry shall become less than nothing before it, till false gods being cast down, mighty systems of idolatry being overthrown, this mountain shall rise above them all, and on and on and on shall this Christian faith grow until, converting into its mass all the deluded followers of the heresies and idolatries of man, the hill shall reach to heaven, and God in Christ shall be All in all." Such is the destiny of the Church; she is to be an all-conquering Church, rising above every competitor.

We may more fully explain this in two or three ways. The Church will be like a high mountain, for she will be *preeminently conspicuous*. I believe that at this period of time, the thoughts of men are more engaged upon the religion of Christ than upon any other. It is true, and there are few that will deny it, that every other system is growing old: gray hairs are scattered here and there, although the followers of these religions know it not. As for Mohammed, has he not become exhausted with gray old age? And the saber once so sharp to slay the unbeliever, has it not been blunted with time and rusted into its scabbard? As for the old idolatries, the religion of Confucius or of Buddha, where is the old activity that made minor idolatries bow before them? They are now content to be confined within their own limit, and they feel that their hour is come that they can grow no further, for their strong man is declining into old age. But the Christian religion has become more conspicuous now than ever it was. In every part of the world, all people are thinking of it; lands once closed to the gospel are now open to it, and soon shall the trumpet voice of the gospel be heard everywhere, and the name of Jesus the Son of the Highest shall there be proclaimed by the lips of His chosen servants.

The hill is already growing, and mark you, it is to grow higher yet; it is to be so conspicuous, that in every village of the world the name of Christ shall be known and feared. There shall not be a Bedouin in his tent, there shall not be a Hottentot in his hut, there shall not be a Laplander in the midst of his eternal snow, or an African in that great continent of thirst, that shall not have heard of Christ. Rising higher and higher and higher, from north to south, from east to west, this mountain shall be beheld, not like the star of the north that cannot be seen in the south or like the "cross" of the south that must give before the "bear" of the north—this mountain, strange to say it, contrary to nature shall be visible from every land. Far-off islands of the sea shall behold it, and they that are near shall worship at its foot. It shall be preeminently conspicuous in clear, cloudless radiance, gladdening the people of the earth. This I think is one meaning of the text when the prophet declares "that the mountain of the Lord's house shall be established in the top of the mountains, and shall be exalted above the hills." This, however, is but a small part of the meaning. He means that the Church of Christ shall become *awful and venerable in her grandeur*.

It has never been my privilege to be able to leave England for any length of time and to stand at the foot of the loftier mountains of Europe, but even the little hills of Scotland, where halfway up the mist is slumbering, struck me with some degree of awe. These are some of God's old works, high and lofty, talking to the stars, lifting up their heads above the clouds as though they were ambassadors from earth ordained to speak to God in silence far aloft. But poets tell us—and travelers who have but little poetry say the same—that standing at the foot of some of the stupendous mountains of Europe and of Asia, the soul is subdued with the grandeur of the scene. There, upon the father of mountains, lie the eternal snows glittering in the sunlight, and the spirit wonders to see such mighty things as these, such massive ramparts garrisoned with storms. We seem to be but as insects crawling at their base, while they appear to stand like cherubims before the throne of God, sometimes covering their face with clouds of mist and at other times lifting up their white heads and singing their silent and eternal hymn before the throne of the Most High. There is something awfully grand in a mountain, but how much more so in a mountain, as described in our text, that is to be exalted above all hills and above all the highest mountains of the earth.

The Church is to be awful in her grandeur. Ah! Now she is despised; the infidel barks at her; it is all he can do; the followers of old superstitions as yet pay her but little attention. The religion of Christ, albeit that has to us all the veneration of eternity about it—"whose goings forth have been from of old, from everlasting" (Mic. 5:2)—yet to men who know Christ not, Christianity seems to be but a young upstart, audaciously contending with hoary-headed systems of religion. But the day shall come when men shall bow before the name of Christ, when the cross shall command universal homage, when the name of Jesus shall stop the wandering Arab and make him prostrate his knee at the hour of prayer, when the voice of the minister of Christ shall be as mighty as that of a king, when the bishops of Christ's Church shall be as princes in our midst, and when the sons and daughters of Zion shall be every man of them a prince and every daughter a queen. The hour is drawing near when the mountain of the Lord's house in her awful grandeur shall be established on the top of the mountains.

There is yet a deeper and larger meaning. It is just this—that the day is coming when the Church of God shall have *absolute supremacy*. The Church of Christ now has to fight for her existence. She has many foes, and mighty ones, too, who would snatch the garland from her brow, blunt her sword, and stain her banners in the dust. But the day shall come when all her enemies shall die. There shall not be a dog to move his tongue against her, and she shall be so mighty that there shall be none left to compete with her. False religious systems shall be hurled like a millstone in the flood. The Church of Christ at that time shall not have kings of the earth to bind and control her, nor shall she have them to persecute her and lift up their iron arm to crush her. But she shall be the Queen of all nations and reign over all kings; she, with her scepter, with her rod of iron, shall break empires in pieces like earthen vessels. She shall say, "I will overturn, overturn, overturn, it: and it shall be no more, until he come whose right it is; and I will give it him" (Ezek. 21:27). The destiny of the Church is universal monarchy. What Alexander the Great fought for, what Caesar died to obtain, what Napoleon wasted all his life to achieve, that Christ shall have—the universal monarchy of the broad acres of the earth. "The sea is his, and he made it: and his hands formed the dry land" (Ps. 95:5). The whole earth shall come and worship and bow down and kneel before the Lord our Maker, for every knee shall bow, and every tongue shall confess that Jesus Christ is Lord to the glory of God the Father (Phil. 2:10–11).

How is this to be done? I reply, there are three things that will ensure the growth of the Church. The first is the individual effort of every Christian. I do not think that all the efforts of the Church of Christ will ever be able to reach the climax of our text. I believe that we shall see something more than natural agency, even though employed by the Spirit, before the Church of Christ shall be exalted to that supremacy of which I have spoken; but nevertheless, this is to contribute to it. Each newly converted believer to Christ does his measure. By the grace of God, let us strive to bring someone else to Christ. In this way, the Church will grow, and as year after year rolls on, each Christian serving his Master, the Church will increase. And it shall come to pass in the last times that even by the efforts of Christ's people, owned by God the Holy Spirit, this mountain shall be highly exalted in the midst of the hills.

This, however, is not all that we have to expect. We can *do* no more, but we may *expect* more. The Church of Christ differs from all other mountains in this fact—she has within her a living influence. The ancients fabled that under Mount Etna, Vulcan was buried. Some great giant, they thought, lay there entombed, and when he rolled over and over, the earth began to tremble, and the mountains shook, and fire poured forth. We do not believe the fable, but the Church of God is like this living mountain. Christ seems to be buried within her, and when He moves Himself, His Church rises with Him. Once He was lying in the tomb, then Zion was but a little hill, then He rose, and day by day as He is lifted up, His Church rises with Him. And in the day when He shall stand on Mount Zion, then shall His Church be elevated to her utmost height. The fact is that the Church, though a mountain, is a volcano—not one that spouts fire but one that has fire within her. And Christ's inward fire of living truth and living grace makes His Church bulge out, expands her side, and lifts her crest, and upward she must tower, for truth is mighty, and it must prevail—grace is mighty and must conquer—Christ is mighty, and He must be King of kings. Thus, you see that there is something more than the individual efforts of the Church: there is a something within her that must make her expand and grow till she overtops the highest mountains.

But remember that the great hope of the Church, although it is reckoned madness by some to say it, is the second coming of

Christ. When He shall come, then shall the mountain of the Lord's house be exalted above the hills. We know not when Jesus may come. All the prophets of modern times have been prophets only from the fact that they have made profit by their speculations. "But of that day and hour knoweth no man, no, not the angels of heaven, but my Father only" (Matt. 24:36). Christ may come while you are reading this word; Christ may suddenly appear in the clouds of heaven. He may not come for many a weary age, but come He must; in the last days He must appear. And when Christ shall come, He will make short work of that which is so long a labor to His Church.

I am looking for the advent of Christ. It is this that cheers me in the battle of life—the battle and cause of Christ. I look for Christ to come, somewhat as John Bunyan described the battle of Captain Credence with Diabolus. The inhabitants of the town of Mansoul fought hard to protect their city from the prince of darkness, and at last a battle was fought outside the walls. The captains and the brave men of arms fought all day till their swords were knitted to their hands with blood; many a weary hour did they seek to drive back the Diabolians. The battle seemed to waver in the balance. Sometimes victory was on the side of faith, and then triumph seemed to hover over the crest of the prince of hell, but just as the sun was setting, trumpets were heard in the distance. Prince Emmanuel was coming, with trumpets sounding and with banners flying, and while the men of Mansoul passed onward, sword in hand, Emmanuel attacked their foes in the rear. Getting the enemy between them, they went on, driving their enemies at the sword point, till at last, trampling over their dead bodies, they met, and hand to hand the victorious Church saluted its victorious Lord. Even so must it be. We must fight on, day by day and hour by hour, and when we think the battle is almost decided against us, we shall hear the trump of the archangel and the voice of God, and He shall come, the Prince of the kings of the earth. At His name, with terror they shall melt, and like snow driven before the wind from the bare side of a mountain shall they fly away; and we, the Church militant, trampling over them, shall salute our Lord, shouting, "Hallelujah, hallelujah, hallelujah, the Lord God omnipotent reigneth."

All Nations Shall Flow Into It

This figure is, perhaps not so sublime, but quite as beautiful as the first. Still endeavor to retain in your minds the picture of this stupendous mountain, reaching above the clouds, seen by all mankind in either hemisphere, a wonder of nature that could not be accomplished by the ordinary rules of art but that divine wisdom will be able to perform. Well, wonder of wonders, you see all the nations of the earth converging to this great mountain, as to a common center. Once in the year all the people of Israel were told to go to the little town of Zion; and now, once for all, you see not Israel but all the nations of the earth coming to this great hill of Zion to worship the Most High God. The white sails are on the Atlantic, and the ships are flying before the wind, even as the bird flits through the sky. What is their noble cargo? Lo, they come from far, bringing the sons and daughters of Zion from the ends of the earth. See you there the camel and the dromedary, the great caravan passing over the pathless desert? What are these, and what is their costly freight? Lo, they are bringing the daughters of God and the sons of Zion up to the Most High God to worship Him. From all parts of the earth you see them coming—from the freezing cold and from the burning heat, from the far-off islands of the sea and from the barren sands, they come, all converging toward the great center of their holy worship. This we are not to understand, of course, literally, but as a figure of the great spiritual fact that all the souls of men shall tend to Christ and to union with His Church.

Again, I beg you carefully to observe the figure. It does not say they shall come to it, but it says they shall *"flow* unto it." Understand this metaphor. It implies first their number. *Now* when our churches are increased, converts drop into the churches; drop after drop the pool is filled, but in those days they shall flow into it. *Now* it is but the pouring out of water from the bucket; then it shall be as the rolling of the cataract from the hillside, it shall flow into it. Now our converts, however numerous, are comparatively few, but then a nation shall be born in a day. The people shall renounce their gods at once. Whole nations shall by an irresistible impulse flow into the Church, not one by one but in one vast mass. The power of God shall be seen in bringing whole nations into the Church of God. You have seen the river flowing onward to the sea, with its banks all swollen, bearing its enormous contribution to the boundless ocean. So shall it be in the last days: each nation shall be like a river, rolling toward the foot of this great mountain, the Church of the living God. Happy, happy, happy day when India and China, with teeming myriads, and all the nations of the earth, with their multitude of tongues, shall flow into the mountain of God!

But the text conveys the idea not only of numbers but also of *spontaneity.* The converts are to come willingly to Christ, not to be driven, not to be pumped up, not to be forced to it, but to be brought up by the word of the Lord, to pay Him willing homage; they are to flow to their conversion. Just as the river naturally flows downhill by no other force than that which is its nature, so shall the grace of God be so mightily given to the sons of men that no acts of parliament, no state churches, no armies will be used to make a forced conversion. "The nations shall flow unto it." Of themselves, made willing in the day of God's power, they shall flow to it. Whenever the Church of God is increased by unwilling converts, it loses strength. Whenever men join the Church because of oppression that would drive them to make a profession of religion, they do not flow, and the Church is weakened and not strengthened. But in those days, the converts shall be voluntarily won—shall come in willingly by divine grace; they shall flow unto it.

But yet again, this represents the *power* of the work of conversion. They "shall flow unto it." Imagine a fool endeavoring to stop the river Thames. He gets into the water, and there he stands, endeavoring to push back the stream. He objects to its flowing toward the sea, and with his hands he tries to put it back. Would you not soon hear laughter along the banks? Ah, fool, to attempt to stop the stream! The word *flow,* here conveys just the idea. "The nations shall flow unto it." The skeptic may rise up and say, "Why be converted to this fanatical religion? Look to the things of time." The false priests may rouse themselves with all their anger to defy Christ and endeavor to keep their slaves, but all their attempts to stop conversion will be like the fool seeking to drive back a mighty stream with his puny hands.

"All nations shall flow unto it." What an idea it is! Take your stand today, like prophets of the Lord, and look into the future. Today the Church appears like the dry bed of a torrent; here I stand, and I see a little water flowing in a secret and threadlike stream among the stones. So little is it that I can barely detect it, but I take the glass of prophecy, I look far onward, and I see a rolling mass of water coming with thundering sound. Wait for a few more years and that torrent, like Kishon's mighty river, sweeping all before it, shall fill this dry bed and swell on and on and on with tumultuous waves of joy, till it meets the ocean of Christ's universal reign and loses itself in God. Here you see, then, that you have more than your imagination can grasp: this stupendous mountain and all the nations of the earth—vast numbers with immense force—spontaneously coming up to the house of the living God.

Is it not a great subject for praise that the nations of the earth *may flow* to the hill of God and to His house? If I were to tell you that all the nations of Europe were climbing the sides of the Alps, you would ask me, "And what benefit do they gain by it? They must pass over the slippery fields of ice, and they may lose their lives in the midst of the bottomless chasms that are overhung by the mighty precipices. They may suddenly be overwhelmed and buried in the all-destroying avalanche, and should they reach the summit, they must fall down exhausted. What is there that men should covet in those barren heights? Rarefied air and cold would soon destroy them should they attempt to exist there." Ah, but it is not so with God's hill. There shall be no snow upon its summit, but the warmth and light of Jehovah's love; there shall be no chasms in its side wherein souls may be destroyed, for there shall be a way, and a highway (the unclean shall not pass over it), a way so easy that the wayfaring man shall not err therein.

Some of the mountains of which we read in Scripture were such that if they were accessible, no one would desire to climb them. There were bounds set round about Sinai, but had there been no bounds, who would have wished to ascend it—a mountain that burned with fire and upon which there was a sound as of a trumpet growing exceedingly loud and long? No, we are not come to a mountain like Sinai with its supernatural thunders; we are not come to a hill barren and bleak and difficult to climb, like the mountains of earth; but the hill of God, though it is a high hill, is a hill up which on hands and knees the humble penitent may readily ascend. You are come to a mountain that is not forbidden to you; it has no bounds set about it to keep you off, but you are freely invited to come to it. And the God who invited you will give you grace to come. If He has given you the will to come, He will give you grace to climb the sides of the hill till you shall reach its upper glories and stand on its summit transported with delight.

While I am writing about the nations that will flow to Christ, might we not weep to think that there are so many people we know who are not flowing to Christ but are going *from* Him? What are the splendors of the millennium to a person if he is Christ's enemy?

For when He tramples His foes in His hot displeasure, the blood shall stain His garments, even as the garments of the winepressers are stained with the blood of the grape. Tremble if you have not come to Him, for the second coming of Christ will be your destruction, though it shall be the Church's joy and comfort. You say, "Come quickly." Do you realize that the day of the Lord is darkness and not light, for that day burns as an oven, and those who are proud and do wickedly shall be as stubble, and the fire shall consume them with burning heat.

You who hear the words of Jesus are invited to come to the mountain of His Church on which stands His cross and His throne. You who are weary, heavy laden, sin-destroyed, you who know and feel your need for Jesus, you who weep because of sin, you are bidden to come now to Christ's cross, to look to Him who shed His blood for the ungodly, and looking to Him, you shall find peace and rest. When Jesus comes with rainbow wreath and robes of storm, you shall be able to see Him, not with alarm and terror but with joy and gladness, for you shall say, "Here He is, the man who died for me has come to claim me. He who bought me has come to receive me. My judge is my Redeemer, and I will rejoice in him." Turn to God! O Lord Jesus, by Your grace, turn every one of us to Yourself!